"Wedding Day Confidence is one of the most enlightening and thought-provoking books we've read as a couple. Hands down, we will always recommend this book to those who want to nurture their relationship and connect on a deeper level."

– Theresa + Rana, co-owners of Attia Events
AttiaEvents.com

"Filled with personal anecdotes, references to psychology, and meaningful concepts, Aaron Daniel's thought-provoking book is applicable not just to all of the engaged couples, but also to the long-married couples of this world. 150 questions that we will certainly continue asking one another for years and years to come."

– Brandon + Dian, cellist and pianist of Luxe Duo, married 2012
LuxeDuo.com

"Captivating and eye-opening... This book made us dive further into our relationship and assess what areas we need to work on. We wish someone had gifted this to us sooner! Recently engaged? Buy this book. Newly married? Buy this book. Oh, and if you're the partner looking to propose shortly... make sure you do three things to be successful.
1. Hire a photographer to catch the moment on camera
2. Get a ring you know they'll love.
3. Buy this book!!!"

– Kevin + Stephanie Douglas, married 2018
Instagram.com/DrStephDouglas
KDCollectibles.ca

"Aaron Daniel Films isn't simply a wedding videographer. He's a magnificent story teller who captured our wedding better than any way we could have imagined. It was personal and beautiful. It told OUR story. With Aaron we gained a lasting friendship far beyond the job. He's passionate about love and you can see it through his work and relationships with others. We are now forever clients of his and refuse to work with anyone else. Seriously he changes the game!!! Don't hesitate and hire him ASAP. So worth it."

– Milana + Srdjan, Hosts of Plant Lana; married 2017
Instagram.com/PlantLana

"Wedding Day Confidence by Aaron Daniels is a well-crafted and insightfully written book. Aaron gave us the tools we need to face not only our wedding day with confidence, but our marriage as well. A remarkable read from a talented storyteller."

– Nich + Sara, co-owners of Bigode Martial Arts and Fitness
BigodeMAF.com

Wedding Day Confidence

150 Questions from a Wedding Videographer to Get You and Your Partner De-Stressed and Smiling on Camera

AARON DANIEL

Aaron Daniel Films

Published 2020 © 2020 Aaron Daniel.

Aaron Daniel Films, Ontario, Canada.

All rights reserved. This book is licensed for your personal use only and may not be sold or given away. No part of this book may be reproduced, displayed, modified or distributed without the prior and express written permission of the publisher.

Designations used by companies to distinguish their products are often claimed as trademarks. All brand names and product names used in this book are trade names, service marks, trademarks or registered trademarks of their respective owners. The publisher is not associated with any product or vendor mentioned in this book.

Limit of Liability/Disclaimer of Warranty: While the publisher and author have used their best efforts in preparing this book, they make no representations or warranties with respect to the accuracy or completeness of the contents of this book and specifically disclaim any implied warranties of merchantability or fitness for a particular purpose. It is sold on the understanding that the publisher is not engaged in rendering professional services and neither the publisher nor the author shall be liable for damages arising herefrom. If professional advice or other expert assistance is required, the services of a competent professional should be sought.

Names: Daniel, Aaron, author.

Title: Wedding day confidence: 150 questions from a wedding videographer to get you and your partner de-streseds and smiling on camera / Aaron Daniel.

Description: First edition. | Ontario, Canada : Aaron Daniel Films, 2020. | Includes Notes and References.

ISBN 978-1-7772761-2-6 (paperback)

ISBN 978-1-7772761-3-3 (pdf)

ISBN 978-1-7772761-4-0 (epub)

Subjects: Weddings. | Family and Relationships. | Self-Improvement.

All inquiries to info@AaronDanielFilms.com
Published by Aaron Daniel Films

Cover Design: Aaron Daniel Films – www.AaronDanielFilms.com

Interior Illustrations: Sam Estrabillo – www.Sam-Estrabillo.com

Table of Contents

Author's Notes   7

Section I: Introduction   9

1. Introduction: Defining good-looking   11
2. The Science: A little film theory, a little psychology   17
3. The Method: The Five A's   25

Section II: The Five A's   35

4. Affection   39

    Questions 1 - 30   47

5. Ambition   71

    Questions 31 - 60   79

6. Artistry   103

    Questions 61 - 90   115

7. Awareness   139

    Questions 91 - 120   147

8. Awakening   171

    Questions 121 - 150   179

Section III: Conclusion   **201**

    9. Conclusion   203

    10. All Questions   207

Acknowledgements   219

About The Author   226

Notes and References   228

AUTHOR'S NOTES

Countless hours spent sitting in the softly lit corners of bookstores have left me with enough stories and lessons on love to tell for a lifetime. Among some of my favourite books, I would meet up with soon-to-be-married couples to plan out filming their special day, and sometimes, I would pick up a title or two to add to my collection on love and the human psyche. It was only a matter of time before I found myself writing my own.

This book is a culmination of rigorous research and curiosity, rooted in over six years' worth of experiences working with couples as a videographer and photographer. Throughout this time, I've become a full-time storyteller, and unintentionally a part-time shoulder to cry on, as I learned to navigate the intricacies of relationships, engagements, and weddings alongside the remarkable couples I've had the pleasure of celebrating love with.

It is this very dedication to learning and exploring love that has informed my practice over the years, allowing me to share real wedding stories on film in an emotionally moving and raw way. It is in sharing experiences with my clients and with you, my readers, that our collective narratives and lessons take on a new breath of life. I've seen the power of having open, vulnerable conversations and how it beautifully translates on camera.

If you picked up this book because you're planning your upcoming wedding, or perhaps you're just curious about how sharing the deepest parts of yourself with your partner can make you look good on camera, then this book is for you. You, too, have countless stories to share. I hope you find yourself in my reflections, the lessons I've learned on the job, and the stories I've had the pleasure of documenting and sharing. The ideas in this book also rely on the knowledge base that therapists, psychologists, marriage counsellors, philosophers and social scientists have built.

Love and art are one and the same. If you know love, you know art.

So, I owe all my art to you, the couple full of love, and to the scientific voices that help unpack the many meanings of love into everyday understanding. This book aims to help you better understand yourself and your partner and learn how to use your chemistry on camera.

The love stories I've shared in this book are of real people and events, however, I have changed sensitive information to protect everyone's privacy. Stories are also an account of moments, and they are subject to the limitations of memory. I have only included the stories that I believe to be true. Yes, I have heard many bridezilla moments, but some are just too wild to be believable.

To all the couples I've had the pleasure of meeting,
to the couples I've yet to meet,
and to those I won't have the chance to,
this book is for you.

- ***Aaron***

SECTION I
INTRODUCTION

1. INTRODUCTION: Defining good-looking

The lights dim in the reception hall, setting the scene for the most defining moment in the couple's life together. A projector flickers images of their first date and first kisses, documenting every moment up to the groom's surprise proposal. As the memories fill the white wall with colour, they welcome a reaction of endearing *oohs* and *aahs* from the audience.

And then came an awkward silence.

Projected for all the wedding guests to see, even the courtesy invites sitting at the back, were photographs of the bride locking lips with none other than the groom's best man.

"Apparently the groom had found out his fiancée was cheating on him and he hired a detective to find out more. When he found out it was the best man, he went along with the wedding... just to expose their secret!"

My jaw dropped to the floor; I couldn't speak.

Moments earlier, I was having a conversation with Stephanie and Kevin about filming their wedding day. Our meeting started with my usual round of questions to get a feel for the type of wedding video they wanted, but the conversation took a turn when we got into things to avoid on the wedding day. Out of nowhere, Stephanie dropped this story they heard from their wedding DJ.

"The groom announced he didn't actually sign any wedding papers, and he told everyone to just have a fun party. The bride's family was paying for everything!"

To this day, my stomach flips every time I think about this story. At the time, I had no reason to believe anything like this would happen outside of a mid-afternoon telenovela. Do couples plan for outlandish catastrophes like this happening on their wedding day?

Anticipatory Anxiety

Whether or not a couple has legitimate fears of soap-operatic plotlines, or something equally rambunctious, playing out, there are more than enough mundane stressors to any wedding day that can keep couples from enjoying their time.

There is a phenomenal amount of stress associated with tying the knot. Given the meticulous planning, tight timelines, and the many moving pieces, there are quite a few reasons why this could be the case on your wedding day. Yet, even if everything goes as planned on the organizing front, couples may have a hard time enjoying themselves. This is often credited to anticipatory anxiety, an overstimulated response to future events and situations. Anticipatory anxiety can lead to preoccupied thoughts, over-exaggeration, and overthinking.

It can be hard to unplug from the worries of your personal, social, and work lives on your wedding day.

Did I choose the right coloured bouquets?

Are the reception seating arrangements fixed?

Is my schedule up to date?

As you celebrate a union and mark a new step in your relationship, it's hardly fair to expect you to be unphased by new responsibilities and commitments you've made to one another, even if it's just for one day. Overthinking takes us all over at some point in our lives. Even wedding guests can get caught up in the rut and feel the strain of the day, even though they are mainly there to party. At some point during your wedding day or videography/photography session, your mind might wander to the things that are annoying or bothering you, and while that's inevitable, it's important to figure out a rhythm that will put you back at ease.

That's what this book is for. Through a series of discussion questions, this book will guide you and your partner to learn more about each of your mind's inner workings, your greatest strengths, and most hindering challenges. These intimate conversations will help you and your partner reconnect and refocus on what's most important—the love you share.

I will also walk you through my framework of getting couples to de-stress and relax on their wedding days (and days after the wedding) so that your videographer can capture the good-looking couple you know you can be on film, all while having a genuinely stress-free time.

But what exactly is "good-looking"?

Perhaps you may envision the mind-boggling "wedding of the year" from *Crazy Rich Asians* or a Hollywood face posing for *Vogue*, but in the next few chapters, you won't find the secrets to becoming the next Golding or Hadid. Instead, you'll discover ways to ensure you share your most genuine smile and loving gaze on your wedding day. And when it comes to capturing your breathless moments with cinematic flair, you can leave that up to your esteemed videographers.

What is Good-Looking?

It was during my pre-wedding meeting with Stephanie and Kevin that I finally was able to contextualize what good-looking truly means for a wedding film.

When first meeting with couples, I like to take the time to get to know them, after all, I won't just be at their wedding, but a part of it. I learned that Stephanie and Kevin's meet-cute took place on the beautiful grounds of the University of Western Ontario. The two kinesiology students were good friends before they started dating and are both from the Southwestern region of Ontario. I also asked what they believe their love languages to be (quality time and acts of service), what song they hear when they envision their wedding video (All The Way's "Timeflies", though their first dance song was Lee Brice's "I Don't Dance"), and what advice they may have for someone planning to get engaged soon ("trust that everything will work out"). Throughout this book, you will understand the importance of asking questions like these, but for now, know that asking the right questions to really understand someone will play a big role in helping them become "good-looking" on camera.

I also asked them my favourite question, "What made my work stick out to you?"

"They're so professionally done, and I just love how there's a story! A lot of wedding videos are just like music videos, but you include the speeches and include such real moments," said Stephanie.

"Ah, like candid shots?"

"Yes! Very candid and real!"

I don't remember her exact words, but that was the gist of her answer. It is also what every bride I've worked with has said to me too. The words "natural" and "candid" are frequent descriptors of what they believe to be a good wedding film.

"I love how you get people's laughs and smiles. And how everything looks so natural. I don't know how else to explain it; it's just so good-looking," she continued as Kevin nodded in full agreement.

"Good-looking," I thought to myself, bookmarking the moment she said it.

The naturalness in my work was good-looking. And it's true, I've seen the way capturing candid, unfiltered, and authentic moments can make a good wedding film. As long as you're genuinely happy, then a good filmmaker will capture authentic good-looking moments without missing a precious second. Even though we use the term "good-looking", it isn't so much about *looking* good as much as it is about *feeling* good.

While that may sound like a simple sentiment, it can be very difficult to achieve. After all, wedding days are known to cause stress and tension. It's absolutely crucial that you and your partner take the time to figure out what makes each of you feel good ahead of your big day.

Looking good requires *feeling* good.

As you proceed through this book, it may help to think like a camera. These days, cameras have digital sensors that capture light and convert our view into an image. If we imagine ourselves as cameras, then the sensor would be our brain and nervous system, which takes in all the stimuli that surround us and interprets information. Just like a camera body, information can only reach us through a lens. Depending on the lens we choose to see the world, we may zoom in and focus too much on the negative details, or perhaps we'll zoom out to get a wide view of life's beauty. Regardless of what may be in front of us, it is the lens we choose to see the world that gives us a scene to remember.

It takes great concentration and practice to focus on something beautiful, but in the end, it's worth it to give your body a full memory card of joy.

As you progress through the chapters together, you'll become more intimately in tune and supportive of one another for when your big day arrives.

In writing this book, I have neatly packaged my approach to filmmaking and the techniques I use to support clients in a five-step process. Coupled with extensive research, intriguing anecdotes, and wild experiences, we'll dive into preparing you and your partner for your wondrous moments on camera.

2. THE SCIENCE:
A little film theory, a little psychology

Dr. Sokalski was a quirky film buff whose humble office set the scene for my early filmmaking days. I always left our weekly student-professor meetings with the sticky aroma of Mr. Noodles on me, his busy computer desk always seemed to hold a fresh brew of instant noodles or soup. I distinctly remember the old VHS tapes along his back wall, just opposite his window overlooking the campus football field. Dr. Sokalski spoke with enthusiasm and urgency to the likes of Tarantino or Scorsese. His quirkiness for film was well-deserved, he always gave the overt impression that he walks the walk to talk the talk. It was a pleasure having him as a mentor and practice-thesis supervisor as I studied film theory and produced my first-ever short film.

"For our project, the one piece of advice for you taking your first directorial role is finding the right actors. There's a saying that goes 'hiring the right actors is half the battle'."

To this day, I think back to this advice.

The right actors are half the battle.

When it comes to wedding films, there is no difference. Good wedding films include characters that know how to play the part, not as fictional personas, but as real people that are in control of the love story they want to tell.

If you're unhappy, people watching will know almost instantly. You might try to fake a smile, but there are so many other ways that your body gives away your emotions. If you've seen the show "Lie to Me" (a favourite of mine back in my teenage years), you know how it's possible to read comfort or discomfort in body movements. According to former FBI agent and body language specialist, Joe Navarro, this nonverbal communication accounts for as much as 80% of what others understand from our messaging.[2.1] Some of us are extremely perceptive at reading these hidden signals, but all of us are capable of reading body language at some level.

We've spent our entire lives learning nonverbal communication. We've learned to read hand gestures that show where to focus our attention, facial expressions that signal disgust, and body posture that signals a lack of interest. Under the scrutiny of a camera, these subtle behaviours can be even more apparent.

Nonverbal communication is complex; without even knowing it, we may signal messages we don't necessarily want to be signalling. We might shake our heads in disapproval, let out a sigh in disappointment or even find ourselves rubbing our temples in confusion without much intention. And what about that time your partner caught you rolling your eyes in annoyance? You may not have said the words 'I'm annoyed', but your neurology is definitely talking.

These gestures stem from our brain's limbic system, which helps us deal with our emotions and is related to the way we trigger our fight-or-flight responses. As proto-humans, if we came across rotten meat, we would crinkle our noses in disgust, signalling to others in our tribe that the meat was no good. This helped the tribe understand the need to stock up on more food. Over the millennia, we've evolved to instantly translate emotions and feelings into behaviour.[2.2]

So, if you're worried about your table décor, or the traffic, or the uninvited wedding guests, you aren't happy. You are inviting a boatload of fake smiles into your big day, and we can tell on camera. You might think you can fake a smile or laugh for the sake of your wedding film, photographs, and guests, but we can all read you. The good news is that we can also read your genuine happiness.

The genuine happiness in a sister's tears while speaking on behalf of their mother in heaven.

The genuine happiness in a father's eyes as he knows his princess is in good hands.

The genuine happiness in a couple's quivering lips as they read their vows of relentless love.

Wedding Stress Stats

Some of you may think, "why does planning my wedding have to be stressful? I know how to get a lot of things done *and* live in the moment!" to which I congratulate you. For many, however, this is not the case.

According to Zola, a wedding planning website, a 2018 study of 500 engaged and newlywed couples showed that 96% of couples planning their wedding were under stress. The majority of these couples (86%) experienced at least three stress-induced physical symptoms, including skin breakouts, hair loss, decreased libido, insomnia, and headaches.[2.3]

This same survey showed that the top three contributors of wedding planning stress are:
1. Budget
2. Perfection
3. Disagreements

Out of these three contributors to stress, perfection is a wedding day stressor that is particularly intriguing. The Zola study described perfection as "the pressure...to look your absolute best and host an Instagram-worthy event". This stressor, then, is the pressure of being good-looking around your guests, but as I'm sure you are now well aware, to be good-looking requires a real stress-free mood.

In order to do this, you must keep your negative thoughts at bay.

The Magic Marriage Ratio

Individuals who frequently think about the negatives in their relationship keep a thunderous storm cloud over their head *and* their partner's. John Gottman found in his research labs with long-term couples that one of the most telling factors for determining an impending divorce is the way a couple defines their history.

Gottman founded a magic ratio that says if you can keep your positive to negative feelings at a ratio of 5:1, you are well-positioned for a lasting marriage of at least 15 years.[2,4] If you experience less than five positive interactions for every one negative interaction, you may be on the way to a divorce lawyer. You want to minimize these negative interactions as much as possible during your marriage, and you surely don't want them to spoil your wedding day.

For the accomplished Hollywood actors, they can channel an inner positivity. They are the ones that know how to draw on their personal memories to bring out a believable action or behaviour. For the short film

I wrote and put together for Dr. Sokalski, it was clear that my volunteer talent had to really grasp the emotions described in the script. The good actors, the ones that you can trust to fight half the film production battle, place themselves in their own history to flesh out the required emotion. For you and your wedding day, we need memories of positivity.

You need to place yourself in an internal theatre of positive memories, reliving those life moments. Those are the feelings you'll need to harness for your wedding day, which will not only make you look good on camera but have a genuinely good time, too.

But how do we do this?

Emotional Memories Can Lead To Automatic Action

We relive our good memories by first knowing them. Some of us have an easy time remembering smells, while others have an easier time remembering pictures. Studies show we all have different methods of establishing memories, but it is our emotions that we can remember most vividly.[2.5]

I always remember the way my siblings and I laughed at Will Smith's eccentric character on "The Fresh Prince of Bel-Air", or how listening to The Fray's "How to Save a Life" still brings back old tears. As the popular proverb goes, "People may forget what you said, but they will never forget how you made them feel."

If those examples don't sit with your history, try thinking of your emotionally intense moments.

The nervousness of presenting at your current job is the same feeling from presenting your third-grade speech.

The fear of losing your grandparents in the middle of a pandemic brings distress in the same way you lost a family member as a child.

The ecstasy of hearing your fiancé's vows is reminiscent of your high school crush also crushing on you.

Did you notice how all these fierce emotional reactions in this present moment are similar in feeling to the emotional reactions you've had in the past? Psychologist Silvan Tomkins's script theory, which he developed in the latter half of the 20th century, explains this observation. Script theory tells us that we create and follow scripts, or procedures, of actions based on the stimuli around us that trigger an emotional response. These scripts are imprinted in our memory throughout our lives.[2.6] For example, if we failed a math test in fifth grade and reacted with signs of shame around our parents, we may react with this same shamefulness as we fail to meet our goals as adults. Effectively, patterns of stimuli that lead to noticeable behaviour are automatic and become even stronger and more automatic the more we give in to these emotional environments or events.

Evolutionarily, scripts helped us make better decisions faster and instinctually. Our scripts can guide us in the right direction without much cognitive energy, like avoiding the smell of rotten meat when looking to cook something. However, scripts can also lead to maladaptive or even negative behaviours, like overreacting in immature ways.

All our past events, whether we are consciously aware of them or not, are still a part of us, lurking in our internal theatres. Both the things we hold onto and the things we may have forgotten can shape the way we interpret and feel emotions today, for better or for worse.

In the next chapter, you will learn my process of analyzing and using your memories to your advantage, creating an authentic smile in the middle of a demanding wedding day. To react happily today, you will learn how to easily draw on your positive memories from your past.

Wedding Day Confidence

3. THE METHOD: The Five A's

As complex as our lives and personalities can be, I propose The Five A's: affection, ambition, artistry, awareness, and awakening, as a way to differentiate and understand the various aspects of our experiences and what makes us who we are. I believe these elements are formed subconsciously during major life stages. They make up how we go about our day-to-day responsibilities and encounters and are an indication of how we act in the world. If we can understand these elements and how they came to be inside us, we can learn to shape them to our advantage.

To do this, you must be ready to reflect on your life and engage in a thorough exploration of your story, willing to shed light on any missing plot-lines. Better still, we will do so with you and your partner. When you master your understanding of The Five A's, you master your ability to emotionally respond to situations, both on and off camera. For the contexts of this book, I want you to imagine how the following five elements in yourself can influence the way you can think positively in front of your partner and your wedding cameras.

1. Affection:

Your ability to trust and develop a healthy attachment.

Those who are naturally affectionate, warm, and can trust others around them are more likely to look good on camera. They know how to form genuine bonds with those around them and can maintain a positive attitude towards others.

Having a strong understanding of one's ways of affection is not only vital to social connection but can also show on camera. Affectionate people often express how important their significant other, as well as their families and social circle, are to their life. They also value independence and self-love, which is indicative of a secure attachment to their independence and co-dependence.

Masters of affection are most notable as emotionally intelligent and empathetic people, such as that friend who always knows just the right thing to say to make you feel better. They connect to each person, as well as themselves, with great empathy and can therefore bring out positive emotions in most situations.

Those who are less affectionate may also be less empathetic. They may sometimes be cold, distant, or completely ignorant of other's feelings or needs. This may have been formed during early childhood and will require the deepest amount of memory digging to understand the current behaviour. The master of affection knows how their environment and early caregivers impacted their ability to express love.

2. Ambition:

Your ability to self-improve and transgress boundaries for growth and development.

The master of ambition knows what moves him in a way that gets his body and mind into gear. He doesn't let the forces of everyday life, the random events and trivial encounters, take control of his internal thoughts and emotions.

For many of us, we understand the importance of being on a goal-driven path, which can take on many shapes and forms. Perhaps you're in pursuit of a pay raise or career advancement or determined to manage your workload to ensure you spend quality time with your future spouse. Whether personal or professional, the element of ambition is our driving force to achieve these goals, but how good are you at controlling your ambition?

Not many of us understand the importance of a balanced ambition. Today's western culture emphasizes and rewards the increased productivity of individuals but often overlooks the need for rest and appreciation.

3. Artistry:

Your ability to create and innovate.

Don't be fooled by the poetic title, everyone has an element of artistry within them, even if they don't consider themselves the most creative individual. For example, the administrative assistant with a knack for organization, the respiratory therapist who understands her mechanical ventilation techniques, and the retail stylist with an eye for aesthetic staging.

The master of artistry understands that his work may or may not sit well with others but knows who to take comments from and how to implement qualifying criticisms. They validate and listen to their higher-ups, picking out any specific insufficiencies. They know when and where to persuade others on their beliefs and their work. And they know how to compromise on the result if ever the scenario should arise. While this is highly relevant to careers, it is the same in a relationship context.

Your dynamic with critique in work is the same as your conflicts in a relationship. The master of artistry understands this and knows how to manage his internal dialogue when experiencing any conflict. The key is to keep a stable relationship.

You will notice that this ability is best formed and moulded during our careers. If we can understand the way we best handle issues at work, we can better handle our relationship issues and promote positivity in our actions.

4. Awareness:

Your ability to connect with society and culture.

The world is becoming increasingly smaller, and those who do well in it know what's going on. They have a pulse on the current global issues, an understanding of the general economy, and an intellectual take on the beauty of many cultures. The master of awareness can harness the world's magnificence and turn it into their own internal world of positivity.

To do this, they sharpen their skills of empathy for the vast array of different people. Fast data, efficient transportation, and global connectedness give them the means to understand people outside their familiar culture. You must do this as well if you want to form strong bonds in your relationship.

For your relationship, the way you are able to empathize and connect with your partner is seen in the way you connect with the world as well. The more you know of the world, the easier it becomes to know your partner's world. Where did they grow up and what was it like? Where did their parents/grandparents grow up, and how has it affected their parenting style? The more you can understand how another's world works, the easier it becomes to empathize and connect on a deeper level.

As we will soon learn, the element of awareness is imprinted on us every time we experience, or travel to, new forms of culture. We can read or watch online as much as we want about other countries or cities, but I truly believe it is in the act of speaking to and living with cultures we currently aren't familiar with that makes us aware.

For most, the freedom to explore the world occurs while we are in our professional career paths and slowly becoming independent of our parents/caregivers. You now have a steady means of providing for yourself, and you may have a partner to take on these worldly adventures with. We will explore this stage of your life during this section of the book and will learn just how important it is in promoting positive attitudes and behaviours.

5. Awakening:

Your ability to realize your place in the bigger world.

The real mastery of positive emotions comes when you complete this stage of element training: awakening. The element of awakening is your inner understanding of your place in the world and the greater universe. It is your ability to be in the *now*.

Eckhart Tolle brought this idea of practicing presence (in his book *The Power Of Now*) to the mainstream and continues to teach his methods of spirituality to the world. His teachings are synonymous with those of past religious and spiritual leaders and can help us understand our place and purpose in the universe. For the purposes of this book, we can understand the element of awakening as our ability to stay self-aware in our daily lives and the greater scheme of the universe.

This may sound a little esoteric right now, but we will soon learn just how present this mindset is in our relationships. Those who are self-aware can easily answer the following questions: how engaged are you with your partner during dinner? How defensive do you get under stress? How insistent are you with winning an argument? Those who are not as self-aware may struggle to reflect on their actions and how they portray themselves to the outside world, often letting their ego get in the way.

As we reach this stage in the book and your life, we can distill the entire process of becoming good-looking in one sentence: openness and acceptance of the present moment allow for positive emotions to set in.

Mastering The Five A's

After developing a better understanding of The Five A's, you can use each element to your advantage so that you can channel your positivity and show your good-looking smile, while helping your partner smile as well. It will become possible to transform the energy spent on stressing on wedding planning, pressures at work, and nervousness of entering a new life stage into more positive outlets. In turn, helping you relax, feel secure, and feel genuine happiness.

When you master all five elements, your life clicks into place. You will develop a better understanding of what will make your relationship thrive, how to empathize with others, and better understand your own emotions.

As we journey through your life history in the following chapters, you will feel confident in yourself, your partner, and your shared path together. If ever there is a time of turmoil or stress, you will think back to this book and know exactly how to handle the situation. It may take some time to master, but you will become the master of your internal theatre and scripts.

In the heat of the moment, you will have the mental techniques to come back into a relaxed and positive state.

Without these techniques, your wedding day can become clouded with pessimism. I have unfortunately seen this happen, and perhaps you have too. While assisting a friend in the industry capture a wedding for Angelo and Connie, we decided to split our efforts. I went to follow the groom in the morning as he got ready, and she went to document the events at the bride's house. I had barely arrived at the groom's house when I get a call, "how's it going over there? Connie is having a few bridezilla moments and I just wanted to make sure you're okay with the guys." I look into the backyard to see the groomsmen having a few drinks; nothing seemed out of the ordinary. As the day goes on, however, I start to notice the nit-pickiness of this bride.

She was constantly asking to make sure things are ready and pointing out the mistakes in the décor. The bridesmaids were getting annoyed, the parents were doing anything to stay away from the wedding party, and the groomsmen, unfortunately for me, could barely crack a laugh or smile. At the end of the night, however, things started to turn around. Different family members began giving their speeches, confessing their true pride and joy for the couple's relationship. No one was talking about the décor or the late arrivals, the speeches were all about the beautiful, positive things people were gathering to celebrate. I started to hear stories of how the couple met, how each family treated the other as their own, and how their friends have nothing less than love and support for the couple. Do you know what happened next? The good-looking tears and relieved smiles take centre stage. Angelo and Connie *finally* let go of all the stress they were feeling, and so did the rest of the wedding party. I rushed to document every good-looking second while thinking, *why didn't they feel this way before the end of the night?!*

This is Angelo and Connie's wedding day story, but it's also a common experience among couples. As soon as couples hear and relive those positive experiences in their lives, a thick wall of negativity comes crumbling down. As we go through the following chapters, you will learn how to break down that wall ahead of your wedding day through a game of 150 questions with your partner.

Your Shared Game

This game is an opportunity for you and your partner to take a guided tour of your lives. It will help you analyze and develop a better understanding of who you are as both individuals and a couple.

Each chapter is specific to one of The Five A's. You will first read an explainer of the element, and then answer a series of questions with your partner.

The questions are intended to facilitate an intimate discussion between you and your partner. I have included statements to explain the significance and relevance of each question to both you and your partner. You will learn why it's important to openly share the answer, and your partner will learn why it's important for them to know. I have also included follow-up discussion questions to facilitate further conversations.

In total, there are 150 questions throughout this book.

If you choose to go through these questions alone, that's perfectly fine. There is no downside to having discussions with yourself. Whether or not you answer these chapter questions with a partner, you will be able to grasp a more thorough understanding of who you are and what it may take to bring your stressful thoughts and actions into a positive light. You do not need to do this with your partner.

The reason this book is formatted for two people is to cultivate a space and time for your relationship to grow. As much as you might be growing together through your daily routines, it can only help you both to carve out time to reconnect with one another. This book will not only help you do that but also prepare for your upcoming big day. The more you invest in these pages, the more you are investing in yourself.

As you and your partner delve deeper into each of your life histories and present realities through The Five A's, the better you will understand each other. It is these moments of emotional and intellectual intimacy that can spark security, closeness, and belonging as a couple. When you master each of the five elements, you and your partner will become master of your internal theatres. You will understand what it takes to let go of any stress and worry and allow yourself into loving behaviour.

Remember, good-looking on camera isn't about posing good, it's about *feeling* good.

Are you ready to feel good?

Wedding Day Confidence

SECTION II
THE FIVE A's

The Five A's

AFFECTION

Wedding Day Confidence

4. AFFECTION:
Early Childhood

> *"It is as if maternal care were as necessary for the proper development of personality as vitamin D for the proper development of bones."*
>
> – John Bowlby

In the late 1960s, a psychologist by the name of Mary Ainsworth conducted a famous experiment on mothers and their 12-18-month-old toddlers. The experiment was done in a lab that mimicked a child's toy room or perhaps a doctor's waiting office.

Ainsworth wanted to find out the different ways children would show attachment to their mothers. At the time of the experiment, there was little known about how our early childhood experiences could dictate how we emotionally attach to others as adults. There were various ideas presented in the field, with some researchers subscribing to the idea that attachment was a more innate genetic characteristic. Ainsworth's experiment helped build the foundation of what we know today as Attachment Theory, which looks at the way we engage in relationships from a psychological, evolutionary, and ethological perspective.[4.1]

Mary Ainsworth, along with John Bowlby, were psychoanalysts who pioneered the use of these early experiments to show that the ways young children developed relationships had an enormous impact on the way they would show attachment and affection as adults. The experiment, the Strange Situation Classification, placed 12-18-month-old children into "strange situations" in the toy room and classified the children based on their reactions. The classifications are still used today and are widely used to differentiate between attachment in adult relationships.

The experiment went as follows:

1. The mother, the baby, and a stranger are in the toy room together.

2. The stranger leaves, now it's just the mother and the baby.

3. Then the stranger comes back and joins the mother and the baby.

4. Now the mother exits the room, leaving the baby and the stranger alone to interact.

5. The stranger leaves while the mother returns to interact with the baby.

6. Now the mother leaves, with the baby completely alone in the room.

7. The stranger returns alone to the baby.

8. Then the mother returns and the stranger leaves.

Strange, right? This could look like a scene out of some kind of psychological horror movie. Thankfully, nothing really strange happened. What *did* happen, though, was a few key observations. Table 1 below:

	Secure Toddlers	Resistant Toddlers	Avoidant Toddlers
When separated from mother	- Distressed behaviour	- Intensely distressed behaviour	- No sign of distress
When with the stranger	- Avoids stranger when alone - Friendly with stranger when mother is present	- Avoids stranger - Frightened by stranger	- Interacts normally with stranger
When reunited with mother	- Happy when mother returns	- Toddler approaches but avoids contact with mother - May also try to push mother away	- Little interest or change when mother returns
Concluding notes	- Toddler relies on mother to perceive safety in environment	- Toddler cries more and is less open to exploring environment	- Toddler is equally comforted by both the mother and stranger
% of Toddlers	70%	15%	15%

Table 1. *Ainsworth was able to classify three distinct reaction styles by the children: secure, resistant, and avoidant. Each column describes the general reaction by each category.*[4.1]

This was a profound study and was the first study to provide empirical data to support John Bowlby's theory of attachment and the childhood effects in our adult relationships. Those who were categorized as "secure" were known to have a secure attachment style, those categorized as "resistant" were known to have an anxious attachment style (sometimes called ambivalent attachment style), and those categorized as "avoidant" were known to have an avoidant attachment style. A few decades after this study, a fourth style, disorganized attachment, was found.[4.2]

Essentially, these early studies showed that babies would later form their adult attachment style based on their mother's sensitivity to their early needs. For example, if a mother was positively responsive to her baby's moods and feelings, that baby would grow to show signs of security in its actions. However, if a mother would respond to her baby's needs in a negative or less-sensitive way, such as showing annoyance or ignoring her baby, the baby would likely grow to react with anxious, avoidant, or disorganized attachment styles. We will soon examine each.

These were important discoveries because it ultimately paved the way for a better understanding of human relationships, the impacts of parenting styles, and helped develop specific treatments and self-care tools for mental health challenges.

Now, let's take a critical look at your childhood and the ways you display affection by examining your own attachment style.

The Four Attachment Styles

The way you interact with your partner, as well as your close friends and family, is determined by your attachment style. Just like the babies in the Strange Situation Classification experiment, when we feel our relationship is at risk, we fall upon our attachment style as a means of dealing with that risk. We each may show signs of all four but tend towards one of these methods of attaching to others:

1. Secure Attachment Style
2. Anxious (or Ambivalent) Attachment Style
3. Disorganized Attachment Style
4. Secure Attachment Style

Anxious Attachment Style:

Evolutionary theories indicate that the anxious attachment style was helpful for the survival of our species. In the past, as we lived in harsher environments, it was a lot harder to stay safe alone. If we wandered off without protection, it was a lot easier to be attacked by other tribes, eat the poisonous fruit, or fall step into predator territory. The anxious individuals would combat this. They would keep an eye on their partner to protect them from harm and stay close enough to pass on their genes. This is the evolutionary roots of the anxious attachment style.

Today, we don't see many tigers roaming Main Street or poisonous hemlock at the grocery store, but we do still hold those same anxious attachment styles. In their book "Attached", Amir Levine and Rachel Heller, two prominent scholars in the field of social psychology, characterize individuals with an anxious attachment style with:

- Being clingy.
- Having intensely persistent and hyper-vigilant alertness towards their partner's actions or inactions.
- Wanting to feel close and intimate with their significant other at all times but tend to overthink whether or not their partner feels the same way.
- Treating their relationships with high stakes and being on the edge of breaking up at the sign of any doubt.
- Being demanding and controlling in their relationship to meet their "good relationship" standard.[4,3]

Avoidant Attachment Style:

On the other end of the spectrum, again on an evolutionary basis, the harsh environments of the past sometimes meant individuals weren't likely to survive long enough to rear offspring. It would have made more sense to quickly move on to other partners, thus the avoidant attachment style.

Today, again through the work of Levine and Heller, individuals with an avoidant attachment style are characterized with:

- Being emotionless.
- Preferring to withdraw from conflicts than address problems head-on.
- Not talking about specific issues with their partner and instinctively resort to saying they don't like them as a whole, grouping any good characteristics into bad ones.
- Prioritizing being independent and self-sufficient as way more valuable than being emotionally intimate or close.
- Finding it uncomfortable to be close and don't like to open up, even if they secretly want to.[4.3]

Where the anxiously attached individual is highly aware of any threat to the relationship, those that are avoidant are very aware and sensitive to any signs of control or imprisonment to their autonomy.

Disorganized Attachment Style:

This is the least understood style. If we take a look at the above examples, we can see the anxious individuals are turning on their "fight" instinct, and the avoidant individual turning on their "flight" instinct. The disorganized individual relies on the third response in our sympathetic nervous system, the "freeze" instinct.

Individuals with disorganized attachment styles are known to freeze under threat and can swing between the behaviours of both anxious and avoidant without reason. This often happens when the ones we love are also the ones that cause us pain. We want to be close, but also understand that they may hurt us. This may come in the form of physical assault, household chaos, or confusing and petty communication (ex. passive aggressiveness).[4.4]

As mentioned, this style is the most recently studied, with one of Amir Levine's students, Dianne Poole Heller, publishing her studies on this style in her book, "The Power of Attachment". She categorizes the disorganized attachment style with:

- Sporadic random shifts in closeness and avoidance
- Misinterpreting threat (e.g. - acting safely in a dangerous environment)
- Misinterpreting safety (e.g. - acting in danger in a safe environment)
- Stubborn and impulsive behaviour
- Low self-esteem[4.4]

This style, coined by Mary Main in 1986, was used to describe infants who grow up in harmful environments with people that bring them fear.[4.2] These children, who may eventually show signs of a disorganized attachment style, may grow up with a confused understanding of what safety and closeness should be like. They instinctively come to fear those who get close and are triggered into a confused freeze, followed by behaviours of anxiety or avoidance.

Secure Attachment Style:

Secure attachment style is, evolutionarily speaking, a consequence of being raised in peaceful environments where parents and children are afforded time to emotionally invest in one another.

Today, individuals with a secure attachment style are characterized by:

- Being naturally warm and loving.
- Open to communicating their problems and letting go of their ego to work things out, as well as being emotionally aware and receptive to their partner's attachment needs.
- They aren't easily upset and can approach things with a rational and emotionally intelligent perspective.
- They understand they can take care of themselves and don't overreact to the things that their partners do or don't do.
- Successes and issues are easily shared with humility.[4.3]

As children, these secure individuals tend to have attentive parents who are good at listening to them and teaching them to express their feelings. These children are often afforded a sense of independence and confidence that allow them health social and emotional development. They can tackle challenges in life without being too needy for acceptance or reassurance and are less distraught by defeat in life because of their strong sense of self-worth.

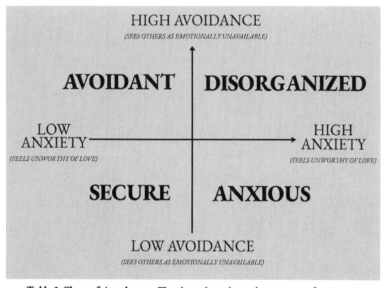

Table 2. Chart of Attachment: The above chart shows the spectrum of anxiety in relation to the spectrum of avoidance.

Now that you have an understanding of how your early childhood can influence your element of affection, let's dive into the specifics of your life. While reading this, you certainly must have connected with one of the attachment styles. While you may react with different types of attachment styles based on the situation you are in, there typically is one form of attachment style that really stands out to each individual.

Are you ready to begin?

Questions 1 - 30

AFFECTION

Q1. Who made you feel the safest while growing up?

As you'll come to recognize with all the questions in this chapter, the above question indirectly gets at the heart of your attachment style. Instead of explicitly asking you what you believe your attachment style is, we will use this time to really dive into the behaviours that you may not necessarily be aware of.

The purpose of this question is to get you to reminisce about feelings of safety from your childhood. It may take a few minutes for you to really think about your past in this way, or it could take as little as a second. For some people, they have a strong inclination to reflect on their past and are already in tune with their attachment system, but for others, traumas during childhood could make this process very challenging. Take all the time you need to open up to your partner. Who does safety look like to you?

For You:

As you and your partner grow together, your partner will take on the role of bringing you the most amount of safety. To do this, they need to know what this looks like to you. The purpose of this question isn't just to share your childhood stories but to help your partner understand your personal ways of feeling loved and cared for. Remember, as a child, you formed your baseline for a "good relationship" based on who you looked towards for love and affection. This caregiver shaped your definition of what love is, whether or not you are consciously aware of it.

Think hard about who you wanted to be around and who you wanted to feel affection from while growing up. Perhaps this was a parent, a guardian, a teacher, or even a neighbour. Name one person, and then start to name a few others that fit this role of a safe caregiver. What was it about this person and these people that made you feel safe? Perhaps it was their comforting hugs, their soothing tone of voice, or their lighthearted, joking attitude.

Tell your partner about the characteristics that really stick out to you and have had an impact on the way you feel safe.

For Your Partner:

Guide your partner into their past with warm eyes and an inviting look of curiosity. As they begin to name the person and people who made them feel the safest, dig deeper into particular interactions. What was it about the person that brought feelings of safety?

Once you get a sense of the person (or people) who brought your partner a sense of safety, try to bookmark their specific characteristics and approach. When times of conflict or stress arise, you can think back to this particular person's personality and approach to bring your partner into safety. For example, if your partner finds safety in comforting words and physical affection, then perhaps you can hold them tight and let them know you are there to support them. Speaking from personal experience, my mother was the one who drew the blueprint for what safety feels like to me. My mother was strong and protective. She was receptive to every little discomfort and feelings of happiness and accomplishment. My Lola (Tagalog for grandma) was like this as well. It's both comforting and clear to see my girlfriend respond to situations with similar characteristics and approaches that make me feel safe. In your relationship, this cultivation of safety is paramount to your loving bond with your partner. Take the time now to discuss ways in which you can cultivate a sense of safety for one another.

For You Both:

Once you understand the characteristics and approaches of early caregivers that brought you safety, it is imperative to keep their memories close to you. When times of conflict or stress arise, you can think back to this particular person's personality and how they interact with you or your partner.

Follow-up Questions:

Q2. What was it about this person or these people that made you feel safe?

Q3. What are the top three characteristics of this person that you want in your partner?

Q4. How would you describe this person's approach to cultivating your sense of safety?

Q5. What action made you feel safe?

Q6. Describe a specific memory of how this person made you feel safe.

Who made you feel the safest while growing up?

Q7. When you needed help, how often did you ask for help?

As we've already learned, our attachment style is imprinted on us in early childhood and often isn't ever acknowledged. But it's still there, subconsciously guiding our every action and behaviour when we're under stress. With this question, the goal is to discuss our tendency towards the avoidant attachment style. How avoidant are we?

When you had trouble doing something as a child, as we all do, was it easy for you to ask for help? When you couldn't reach the cupboard for a cup of water, did you find yourself building a ladder out of chairs and stepping stools and monkey-ing your way to the high shelf? Or did you open up for help? For the avoidant children, becoming builders was the more obvious option.

These avoidant individuals were so used to being alone or feeling emotional neglect that relying on others seemed out of the question. Maybe it was an absent father who seemed to choose work over you, or a mother who was forced to take the double-shift to pay this month's rent, or an older sibling who just wanted to look cool in front of all her friends without you. Someone may have been there to teach you how to do something, but you couldn't grasp the idea of relying on anyone for support.

For You:

Does this sound like your childhood? That's okay. With your partner, I want you to think deeply about all the feelings of inattentiveness growing up.

Where were you?

What did you need?

When did you have to hold back the tears?

Describe these scenes to your partner, as slowly as you may need, and accept that this happened.

For Your Partner:

It's important to keep your partner feeling safe, as recalling memories like these can be quite challenging. If you feel they need space, give them room to breathe and process their thoughts and emotions. However, remember that they need to feel you there, so reassure them of your presence and your protection.

Guide them through their childhood scenes as if they were watching a movie of themselves. Help them feel and fully explain the emotions of their younger selves.

For You Both:

When the time is right, look into your partner's eyes. Emotional presence through prolonged eye contact is shown to promote a deeper connection. I first came across the following visualization technique through the work of Diane Poole Heller:

Pretend you are still that lonely child, desperately wishing you didn't have to do everything yourself. Keep looking at your partner as they smile at you with a caring look. Neither of you needs to speak.

Now pretend those eyes were looking at the child version of you. Imagine you went back in time to when you needed help, and now your partner is there. Smiling at you, helping you, showing you affection. You feel them there, and you feel safe.

You smile back.

Now you're back to the present, needing help with something new, and you feel overwhelmed. But now you have your partner's eyes still locked on you. They're here for you now, too. Smiling at you, helping you, showing you affection. You feel them here, and you feel safe.

Heller coined this as the Corrective Experience exercise.[4.4] It is meant to recreate a perfect welcome into the world as you take on tasks with an affectionate caregiver. In this example, we used your partner as that caregiver, but this exercise can also be envisioned with anyone who brings you feelings of appreciation and closeness.

When stress arises, remember this exercise. You aren't alone, and you don't need to do everything alone. When you open up to your partner about your feelings of tension or nervousness, it tends to become easier to take on the obstacle. You can succeed together.

Follow-up Questions:

Q8. Describe an early memory where you under stress and had to solve a problem on your own.

Q9. If possible, describe something you were taught as a child that you felt had unsatisfactory guidance.

Q10. Share a specific memory of when you needed the most help from someone else.

Q11. Practice the Corrective Experience exercise.

Q12. Clearly invite your partner to feel an empathic pain or stress you currently have and accept that they are there to help.

When you needed help, how often did you ask for help?

Q13. When did you feel anxious in your relationships?

If you identify with the anxious attachment style, it may be easy to see how your past relationships lead you into various cycles of anxiety. Were you frightened when your mom was late picking you up from school? Did nervousness creep into your life every time your dad didn't pick up the phone? This question is intended to help you and your partner understand your ambivalent attachment style and discuss ways of mitigating these feelings in the future.

As a reminder, the ambivalent attachment style shows in the extreme need for reassurance. There's a tendency to over-think and ask questions to make sure everything is still in the state we expect it to be in. There's a looming fear of loss and the feeling that something is bound to go wrong. Although people with anxious attachment styles tend to focus a lot on their partners, this tends to come off as being overprotective and untrusting.

In early childhood, these ambivalent reactions stem from the absence of consistent affection. Perhaps your mother's schedule didn't allow her to pick you up from school at consistent times or maybe your primary caregiver was only allowed in the country a few months of the year for work.

The unpredictability we felt as kids can lead us to many negative thoughts. On a subconscious level, we began to feel insufficient or too inadequate to deserve the affection we all needed. We might subconsciously think, "my dad never wanted me, so when I feel love, I'm going to keep it as close to me as possible." We longed for it, so we may obsess over it.

In a research experiment, a pigeon was caged with a food dispenser. Every time the pigeon hit the bar on the dispenser, it would receive a food pellet. The pigeon would hit the bar until it was no longer hungry. This was a secure-sounding pigeon. Then the researchers switched the pellet dispenser to only release food at irregular times. When the pigeon hit the bar, sometimes it would receive food and sometimes it wouldn't. The pigeon then became obsessed with hitting the bar. When it expected being cared for, sometimes its needs were ignored, which led to obsessive behaviour. What the researchers found was that intermittent rewards, much like gambling and much like our unpredictable caregivers, can lead to anxious behaviours.[4,5]

For You:

Does this sound like your childhood? Do you remember those afternoons just waiting at your grandmother's door waiting to be picked up by your parents? Or anxiously making sure your parent or guardian is still in the house? The goal here is to understand your earliest forms of anxiousness to paint a picture of your current anxieties.

Think hard and deep about your childhood worries and what relationships led you to these feelings of anxiety. Be as open and honest as you can as you answer this question. Again, the purpose of this question is to help you and your partner understand what types of scenarios influence your anxious behaviour the most.

For Your Partner:

Safety is a priority when it comes to early memories like this. Unlike our avoidant memories that promote low or sad emotions, our ambivalent memories can promote high-energy or angry responses and emotions. Be aware of this as your partner may start to become hyper-aware of their surroundings. Remember to keep them calm and feeling safe.

For You Both:

When you can both understand the specific ways that anxiety creeps into your lives, it becomes easier to tackle. Especially when you're fighting as a team. As you go through your early history of ambivalence and anxiousness, take note of any patterns. How did you behave, and why?

The severity of our actions, while anxious, may cause issues in our relationships. The best way that I've found to handle these emotions is by practicing an abundance mindset.

An abundance mindset can mean a lot of things to many people. For the context of this book, this practice describes our ability to see beyond the current situation, especially negative ones. It encourages us to realize that there is so much to be positive about and appreciative of.

For example, Dr. Diane Heller tells the story of a woman who believes the only men she attracts, who describes are too busy with work, are incapable of giving her the attention she needs. As Dr. Heller delves deeper into the challenges her client is facing, the woman starts to open up about her 2-year relationship. At first, it was described as being inattentive and unpassionate. Then, the woman admits that her boyfriend does go out of his way to plan intimate dinner dates every time he comes back from a work trip. Among other realized examples, the woman starts to smile and agree that her relationship isn't as bad as she kept telling herself.[4.4]

In your situation, actively find the good. Maybe it's your feeling of unpreparedness that brings anxiety—in which case your partner could find ways to reassure you that you are indeed prepared. Or perhaps it was the memories of feeling small—in which case you could remind yourself of your strength and courage. Or maybe the thoughts of being weird or different—which you could argue by showing love for uniqueness and individuality in others and yourself. When you or your partner start overthinking situations, actively practice your thoughts of abundance.

Sometimes you might feel the tense pressures of wedding planning, or job hunting, or housebuilding, but just like the feelings of neglect you get from time to time, practicing an abundance mindset can do wonders for your stress levels.

Everything will be okay, and you can trust each other to find and make the best out of anything.

Follow-up Questions:

Q14. Would you describe yourself as overly frightened when your caregivers were unavailable?

Q15. Was there a lot of unpredictability during your childhood?

Q16. Thinking back, do you remember being overly obsessive about certain things as a child? Explain.

Q17. If applicable, describe a childhood memory that still makes you angry today.

Q18. What reoccurring events happen when you feel anxious today? Describe these patterns to your partner, as well as how you can implement an abundance mindset to mitigate this feeling.

Q19. Is there anyone you were really close with, but now feel confused about how they treated you?

This question gets at the heart of the fourth and final attachment style—disorganized attachment. Recall that individuals of this style desperately want to feel close relationships but also tend to fear intimacy at the same time. They switch from the extremes of ambivalent and anxious attachment to the extremes of avoidant attachment. This confusing system often shows itself in the form of freezing (too confused to know what to do). Clearly, acting in this way can be very upsetting to your relationship, especially because it goes from one extreme to the other.

As we look to our past, we can attribute this disorganized attachment behaviour to our confusing environments. The people and places we were supposed to feel safe with were actually the people and places that inflicted pain in us. We wanted to feel the love from someone, but they ended up hurting us.

Maybe it was during recess when a group of friends didn't really treat you like a friend. Maybe it was a teacher who you felt made fun of you. Maybe it was the thought of a creepy old piano teacher you didn't want to play for. In all cases, there was a caregiver that you felt the need to trust and gain affection from but would treat you in hurtful and fearful ways. If the disorganized attachment style relates most to you, you have grown up with a confused understanding of what closeness should be like.

It's a constant battle between feeling affection and feeling endangered. When these individuals grow up, they instinctively come to fear those who get close and are triggered into a confused freeze, followed by behaviours of anxiety or avoidance.

Is there anyone you were really close with, but now feel confused about how they treated you?

For You:

If your early memories lead you to believe you have a disorganized attachment style, you are not alone. Although this is the newest and most misunderstood of the four attachment styles, many researchers have identified this style in many relationships. This style of attachment also resonates with many of the couples I've worked with. At the beginning of their relationships, these couples describe experiencing extreme moments of falling in love, followed by moments of suffocation. When put into stressful situations, like planning a party or making a big purchase together, there is a flux between hyper-anxiety and lackadaisical care. One second they're overthinking, and then the next second they're not caring at all. This is not often perceived as a healthy way to handle challenges.

Remember, these subconscious behaviours can change, and it starts by acknowledging them. Now is the time to address some ways to diffuse these behaviours.

For Your Partner:

Your ultimate goal is to help your partner regulate their emotions and bodily reactions. If they grew up adopting a disorganized attachment style, then they may face challenges interpreting affection, often confusing it with danger. The opposite is true as well—they might feel the safest while in dangerous situations. For example, they may subconsciously choose to walk through dangerous parts of the city or being in hostile environments.

You must realign their feelings of affection with their body's interpretation of safety. To do this, as in our previous questions, ask your partner what helps them feel safe and act accordingly.

For You Both:

Reflect on what safety looks like and feels like. Remember that you and your partner are now a source of safety and security for one another.

When one of you begins to feel a sense of dysregulation in the other, stop what you're doing and address it right away. Some couples have a secret code that lets the other know that they are slipping into disorganized behaviour.

If your partner begins to breathe heavily into a flustered state of anxiousness or avoidance, come up with techniques that you can use to support your partner. Some codes couples can use include touching their feet together, hand gestures, or even standing in a particular place in the house. These cues let your partner know you are trying to get them into a safer emotional state and that everything will be alright as long as you continue to hold a safe space for one another.

Take the time now to come up with your secret code. For example, whenever I start to feel anxious or too avoidant, my girlfriend will grab me by the face and touch our foreheads together. It's a little too embarrassing to do in public, but the humour in staring at each other as we touch foreheads has always brought me comfort. I'm laughing just as I write about it.

Follow-up Questions:

Q20. Are you still holding on to these confusing childhood relationships?

Q21. Describe a childhood memory of yourself actively going into a dangerous situation.

Q22. What one situation, in your early childhood, caused you to feel the most loved one second, followed by the most hurt the next second?

Q23. When do you feel the most frozen to act on stressful situations?

Is there anyone you were really close with, but now feel confused about how they treated you?

Q24. Come up with a secret code that you and your partner can use to indicate the other is slipping into a behaviour of insecurity.

Q25. Where in the world would you like to live?

We've learned about the four attachment styles, what secure affection feels like, how insecure styles can show itself in our relationships, and how you, as a couple, can find ways to diffuse their negative impacts. Acknowledging the consequences of these early memories is the first step to healing our current insecurities—like emphasizing our acts of security with one another, creating an atmosphere of trust and belonging, and creating ways to remind each other of this affection. Remember, practicing these consistently can be a big difference in the long-term.

Being open to these changes in our thought process may be a challenge to us. Where in the world would you like to live? This question aims to create openness between you and your partner through conversations about your dream home together.

For many, the idea of a future home is a dream that gets built from childhood. When you were young, you probably saw many neighbourhoods and homes that really stuck out to you. The ones that you came to admire must have left an imprint on your mind. You've seen many places throughout your life, and you probably have a good idea of what a "good" home is. With this question, the goal is twofold: to get a clearer understanding of your ideal environment to feel love and to understand how open you are to include your partner in your lifelong dream.

For You:

The first part of this question brings us back to the first question in this chapter, "who made you feel safest growing up?"

In that question, you learned of your early ideas and definitions of what love feels and looks like. In this question, we now try to bring these feelings into the present. Where, based on the places you enjoyed as a child, would you like to live in the present day? This part doesn't have to be too descriptive; the objective is solely to bring your past into the present.

Think about your family vacation. Your early trips to different cities or states. What architecture really stood out to you, and what was the weather like? This could be any place throughout your life, not necessarily limited to your early childhood. The idea here is to bring up past longings that your partner doesn't necessarily know already.

For Your Partner:

The second part of this question is where we will try to understand your place in your partner's dream home. As your partner describes their house and their neighbourhood, guide them into how they see you fit into that dream.

Some people spend a lot of time imagining where they want to live, and others are not as attached to a specific idea of a dream home.

If your partner is very attached to their idea of what they want their home to look like, they may not have acknowledged your place in that dream just yet. Ideally, this question brings any uncertainty each of you may have into the open.

Do they clearly see you beside them?

Are you both available for each other in this future?

Does each of your personal goals align?

This question should spark conversations about how open each of you are going to adapt your dreams in a mutually beneficial way. How accommodating is your partner to your needs?

If your partner isn't strict to the idea of the perfect dream home, chances are they are open and accepting of the change. This is good and shows their adaptability to change. If you do sense even the slightest form of hostility, this is a good place to pause and have a discussion.

For You Both:

As a couple, you are part of one unit. Studies have shown that the reliance couples develop on one another is not only an emotional bond but a physiological connection as well. Couples, quite literally, can influence one another's bodies.[4,5] This includes blood pressure, heart rate, breathing, and even hormonal levels. Given this influence on one another and how intertwined your lives can become, you need to act as a team. This means always addressing each other's needs with openness.

Discussing your home together is a lighthearted way to address one another's needs. You may have different preferences for pillows and absolutely hate your partner's choice of cutlery but as you begin to find compromises in the little things, you'll carve the path for encouraging openness elsewhere in your relationship. When you feel comfortable coming to agreements on the little things, like a new wall colour or a placement of a piano, it becomes easier to have heavier discussions and make more difficult decisions together.

Agreeing on a wall colour could lead to agreeing on immediately starting a conversation when feeling avoidant, instead of running away.

Agreeing on a table set could lead to agreeing on hugging each other when you begin to sense feelings of disorganized behaviour.

Agreeing on the placement of the piano could to lead agreeing on saying "I love you" more often.

Cultivate your relationship with these open discussions. Start small if you need to and understand the ways you best come into alignment with your ideas and needs.

When we sift through the many fish in the sea, it is our chosen partner that becomes both our grounded path and guiding signs. We must learn to trust them. As those partners, we must learn to help the relationship weather any emotional storms.

Follow-up Questions:

Q26. On a scale of 1 to 10, how happy are you with the attachment style you believe to have?

Q27. On a scale of 1 to 10, how much do you think you need to work on your attachment with your partner?

Q28. Describe a pleasant environment you frequently visited as a child.

Q29. How clearly can you see your partner in your dream home?

Q30. On a scale of 1 to 10, how flexible do you believe yourself to be when it comes to meeting your partner's needs in a future home?

So which baby were you in that Strange Situation experiment? And which attachment style do you have today?

Secure?

Avoidant?

Ambivalent?

Disorganized?

Whichever one tends to show itself in your relationship, the important thing to note is that you have each other. As a team, it is your mission to use the techniques you've learned to master your understanding of the first of The Five A's—the element of affection.

As you've already experienced, affection helps your inner theatre stop playing your negative memories and promotes your positive ones. Immerse yourself in those happy moments, and you will confidently become a master of affection in yourself and with others.

STOP – Before moving forward:

How would you rate your element of affection?

☐ 1 ☐ 2 ☐ 3 ☐ 4 ☐ 5 ☐ 6 ☐ 7 ☐ 8 ☐ 9 ☐ 10

How would you rate your partner's element of affection?

☐ 1 ☐ 2 ☐ 3 ☐ 4 ☐ 5 ☐ 6 ☐ 7 ☐ 8 ☐ 9 ☐ 10

Rapid Action Steps:

1. Write down the number one area in your life that needs the most improvement with your element of affection (e.g. - Speaking, listening, behaving).

2. Every morning for the next week, wake up and tell yourself that you are going to act with better affection in this area of your life.

3. Read the Aaron Daniel Films blog section on relationships: https://aarondanielfilms.com/blog/category/On+Relationships

The Five A's

AMBITION

Wedding Day Confidence

5. AMBITION:
Internal Progress

"Imagine that in order to have a great life you have to cross a dangerous jungle. You can stay safe where you are and have an ordinary life, or you can risk crossing the jungle to have a terrific life. How would you approach that choice? Take a moment to think about it because it is the sort of choice that, in one form or another, we all have to make."

– Ray Dalio

Ambition is the element that drives us to succeed, the fire within us that pushes us to achieve our goals. To illustrate how ambition works, we first need to understand that personal evolution towards success has five major steps, depicted here:

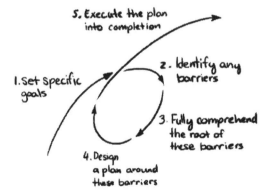

Figure 3. The Five-Step Process of Personal Evolution: *There is a general procedure to reach our goals. A five-step process, which Ray Dalio, billionaire and founder of the world's largest hedge fund, promotes as his "5-Step Process to Get What You Want Out of Life".* [5.1]

I could have used multiple historical figures and fictional characters to illustrate the stages of success: Don Vito Corleone from "The Godfather", Rocky, Steve Jobs, Eminem, Dr. Dre, Walt Disney, Chris Gardner from "The Pursuit of Happyness". These are just a few rags-to-riches stories that most of us are familiar with, but none of them had a strong emphasis on their romantic relationships.

Then I heard the perfect story.

I was sitting with a groom's grandfather in his basement, and he was casually telling me childhood stories from the '50s and '60s. And then he started telling me about his immigration journey to Canada.

With a concentrated expression on his face, he tried to recollect his memories to tell the story.

Implementing The Five Steps of Ambition

Step 1: Set specific goals

"When I graduated from high school in the Philippines, my family wanted to send me to college and study agriculture. We had a farm and it's all that we knew, but my parents wanted me to pursue higher education because it would lead to a better life."

He grew up in Mayantoc, a small village where houses barely had electricity and, to this day, can be described as concrete shacks. The housing was so dense and packed that if it wasn't for the friendly community that lives there, it would've been a very chaotic neighbourhood to grow up in. Just outside of this village was his family farm. As a child, he had very supportive parents that wanted to see him grow beyond life on this farm, so they enrolled him in a college about two and a half hours away.

on the farm

Step 2: Identify any barriers

Once he found a place to live near the college, he was forced to make payments he was not prepared to make. His older sister had just taken a job as a full-time teacher and was very adamant about helping him with the expenses. His whole family wanted him to succeed. As the first month passed and the expenses started to pile up, he realized that he and his sister could no longer afford his education. So he packed his bags and moved back home.

His father was outraged and even suggested selling their family farm.

"Don't do that, father. My education can wait. I'm still young. Sister Pat could be better off after a year. And if not, I will find my way. I am going to acquire my higher education by myself, not by selling anything."

Step 3: Fully comprehend the root of these barriers

As time went by, he spent his early twenties going from one job to another. He worked in construction, on a friend's farm across the country, delivered rice, and at some point, even considered getting into professional boxing. But he knew he would eventually have to pursue higher education.

Throughout all these jobs, he eventually realized a big mistake in his thinking. All these opportunities were leading him down dead-ends because he lacked formal experience. Without the proper qualifications, whether that be experience or a degree, he would continue to be stuck in this circle.

Eventually, he landed a full-time position as a security guard. This is when his life started to turn.

as a security guard

Step 4: Design a plan around these barriers

As a security guard, he prioritized learning as much as he could about the job and the properties and people he was protecting. One of these properties was a car repair shop. He would spend the day with the mechanics, bringing along books on automotive repair and learning from them as they fixed cars. When nightfall came, and the mechanics left to go home, he stayed behind to fulfil his nightly guard duties. At this point in his life, he was married and was looking forward to the arrival of his first child, but he also felt the pressure of needing to provide more for his family. The security guard position was not enough.

The car shop owner learned of his interests and eventually hired him to work in the shop. He went on to gain hands-on experience but knew he needed to continue growing in order to achieve his higher goals of finding a life outside of his family farm.

Step 5: Execute the plan into completion

He never stopped pursuing opportunities for growth. He started working full-time on mechanical installations, then electrical servicing, repair, and production. With steady pay and established experience, it may have seemed like higher education wasn't part of his plans anymore, but it always was at the back of his mind.

Eventually, he enrolled and completed a two-year combustion engine technician course at the nearby university. He passed at the top of his class with a full scholarship reimbursement on his tuition fees. He finally fulfilled his promise to his parents to pursue higher education, but he didn't stop there. He knew his potential and went on to get a teaching degree to cement his professional qualifications.

As luck would have it, an old classmate of his informed him that a recruiter from Canada was sponsoring mechanics wanting to immigrate. He was hesitant at first, assuming that the only people being recruited would have connections to the immigration system. He decided to apply, not willing to pass up a possibility that could lead him and his family towards his goals at a better life.

After three days of completing an exam and applying alongside 2000 applicants, he got his acceptance letter. He was one of 14 people accepted.

A few months later, on May 10, 1975, he moved his family to Hamilton, Ontario. Here, he grew his influence at the Dofasco factory while raising four kids who went on to pursue successful engineering and teaching careers. Now a grandfather, he looks back on his life and realizes that he fulfilled his goals of creating a better life outside the farm.[5.2]

This is ambition.

settling into Canada

Ambition is taking every ounce of your experiences and channelling it into achieving your goals. Ambition is knowing where you want to be in the future and cultivating your inner fire to get you there.

The past groom in this story was my cousin, and his grandfather is my grandfather. Lolo Marino has been, and always will be, an inspiration for the ambitious growth of my family. Without his drive to provide for himself and my grandmother, this book would not be here.

Ambition, the second of The Five A's, is riddled throughout many origin stories. Although this particular example hangs on the experience of immigration, everyone can learn something from it.

Highlighting Your Ambition

Ambition is an element that some of us let shine more than others, but we all have this internal drive within us. When it comes to your love life, your ambitiousness has a drastic influence on the way you tackle problems and conflicts within your relationship.

Just like Lolo Marino, you need to strategize a solution and follow through on your designed plans. And just like his hard-working and always-learning personality, this needs to be done with skill.

Maybe your goal was to find the perfect wedding planner that fits your budget, so you set out a plan to do so. Or maybe it was the goal of secretly proposing to your partner, so you found a way to do so. Whatever goals you have in life, it is your element of ambition that gets you there.

In the following questions, we will delve into each of the above five steps and learn how strong you and your partner's sense of ambition and drive truly are. This is imperative to your relationship, as your growth together relies not just on affection, but the ambition to keep growing together. You feel this through achieving goals as a unit, learning from and with one another, and helping one another achieve individual and mutual success. Consequently, this mutual growth will only enhance the positives in your life.

This chapter will take us into the next life stage after early childhood. It is in our grade school days that I believe we begin to cultivate our sense of ambition. It is during this time that we start to develop independence from parents and guardians.

Ambition is the first step to mustering the strength to create our own decisions in life. Just like the challenges my grandfather faced, we too start to fend for ourselves and make decisions for growth. Perhaps your goal is to move to another country or maybe to secure a safety-net of income for your growing family. Whatever your goals are, let's find out how to best achieve them and grow your element of ambition.

Questions 31- 60

AMBITION

Q31. Who was living the life you wanted to live?

As we start to imagine your life's ambitions, this question aims to shed light on your teen and pre-teen idols. In this chapter, we will also look at your ability to achieve your goals and what progress you've made so far.

This question is a conversation starter for the first step ("set specific goals") in Ray Dalio's "Five-Step Process to get what you want out of life" (see Figure 3). During our adolescence, we looked up to others and often perceived them as role models. In a way, these models were also our subconscious goals. How did you determine these role models, these goals?

For You:

Maybe you wanted the acting potential of Daniel Radcliffe. The voice of Carrie Underwood. The skill of David Beckham. Or perhaps you wanted the wealth of Scarface (without the notorious crime record, of course). Whoever it was, think hard and deep about your early idols.

Paint a picture for your partner. Describe what you wanted to see in the mirror as a soon-to-be adult. Then, explain why you wanted to be like these people.

Often, we place a goal in our minds that isn't actually a goal. They're just desires. And the difference between a goal and desire, as Ray Dalio describes it, is that a goal is something you absolutely *need* to achieve, and a desire is just a *want* that can get in the way of success.

The second common hurdle of goal setting is having too many goals and too many people you wished to mimic. Yes, we are all influenced by everyone around us, but if you let yourself take influence from too many people, you will start to see contradictions in your goals. You might want the social media fame of YouTuber Logan Paul and the book credentials of famed author Yuval Noah Harari. Clearly, these are very different goals, with one requiring an indefinite amount of energy for the camera and the other an indefinite amount of concentration on historical literature and modern society. You can achieve anything you want, not everything you want. Stay focused because, like the advice of many successful entrepreneurs, the riches are in the niches.

For Your Partner:

As your partner describes their idols growing up, make sure to ask probing questions to get at the root of why they looked up to these people. Remember, if your partner only admires someone without learning anything specific from them, then these individuals aren't role models for goals, but possibly just desires.

For example, your partner may say that they looked up to Cristiano Ronaldo. What is it about Ronaldo that your partner learned from them and aspired to achieve? His athleticism? Political awareness? Philanthropy? GQ physique? Keep probing your partner for their full story. You could ask things like what were you doing when you pictured yourself in their shoes? When would you have liked them to take over for you?

For You Both:

If you find that you and your partner don't have clear goals, be honest with yourselves. And if you find yourselves having met your goals too frequently, consider raising the bar and aiming higher. Meaningful and impactful goals take time to complete.

It's in your best interest to learn from any habitual mistakes. As you continue your life in unity with many goals to come, be ready to hone in on your specific needs as a couple. Do you want fame? Talent? Wealth? Love? Respect? If so, why?

With your growing affection, come to a mutual understanding of what your goals should be. This will sharpen your element of ambition, both individually and together.

Consequently, the better you are at setting goals, the easier it becomes to achieve them.

Follow-up Questions:

Q32. Do you believe you set goals too much for the short-term or for the long-term?

Q33. Were you trying to be like too many people?

Q34. Thinking back, do you think you were confused about the look of success and what you believe to be success today?

Q35. How easy was it to achieve the goals you wanted?

Q36. In what grade school situations would you have liked your idol to take over for you?

Who was living the life you wanted to live?

Q37. What aspects of yourself do you wish you worked on more?

When I think back on my elementary school days, there are many things I would have done differently. For starters, I would want more confidence in myself so that I could experiment and learn from my mistakes. Growing up, I was often afraid of getting negative feedback. I would make the mistake of setting the bar as low as I could get away with. This kept me in stagnation and ultimately held me back from feeling any sense of accomplishment.

Answering this question helps you get at the heart of the second step in the five-step process: determining barriers. And just as a reminder, we use our past as our indicator of how we do things currently. When you were a grade-schooler, was it easy for you to determine your barriers, or do you think it was hard?

A lot of us have a myopic attitude towards the obstacles in our way. This attitude needs to change because determining what our obstacles are is necessary to conquer them. For example, if you planned to walk up a hill without giving any attention to the black ice that covered it, you won't wind up going anywhere (unless it's the ER because what you did there is quite dangerous). The barrier in this scenario is the ice. If you were oblivious to its presence, you won't know what is preventing you from walking up the hill. So, the first step across the ice, across this barrier, is to be aware of the obstacle in the first place.

For You:

When you think back to the problems you had in grade school, do you think you handled them well? Put yourself in your younger self's shoes. Perhaps you were worried about finishing an essay, an art project, or a science presentation. What was stopping you from completing this goal?

As your younger self, how would you have answered?

"I don't have enough time."

"I'm not smart enough to do it well."

"I can't do it alone."

All of these excuses could be traced to procrastination and a lack of self-discipline. I know this because that was me. I still procrastinate, but since I'm aware of it, it's easier to diffuse. And self-discipline takes time and maturity.

The important thing is not to give in to these barriers. Don't give into believing there's not enough time and make the best use of it; don't give in to a lack of knowledge and find out what you need to know; don't give in to feeling helpless and ask for support.

For Your Partner:

If your partner can clearly illustrate what their barriers were, and what aspects of themselves they wished to work on more, this is a good sign. Self-awareness is a good indicator of growth. However, if they seem to be shy of reliving their past problems and past barriers, they may have a hard time acknowledging their current barriers as well.

To help your partner tackle any current obstacles, practice a polite openness. Be open with them about what you see as a barrier for them. Having your second opinion and perspective can bring clarity to any situation. Perhaps they think their income is the problem when you think it's actually their spending habits. Maybe your partner thinks they need to read one more book, but you're sure they're ready to start writing their own.

We will dive into this polite critique in the next chapter, but for now, understand that you are your partner's accountability partner. Help them see what they can't see.

For You Both:

Obviously, you both can't know everything, but two heads are always better than one. Practice polite openness and honesty with each other when it comes to individual goals and barriers. Sharing your interpretations and perspectives on an issue will only build a deeper understanding of any challenges you may be facing. The more focused and defined a barrier is, the easier it becomes to overcome it.

At the end of the day, you both want to have a good understanding of each other's internal and external obstacles. As you grow (and struggle) together, it is both your individual confidence and your intricate teamwork that will help you achieve your goals through a shared understanding of problems.

Follow-up Questions:

Q38. Do you believe it was hard for you to determine what stopped you from achieving your goals?

Q39. Do you think you handled your problems well?

Q40. What stopped you from achieving your goals as a young adult?

Q41. When you are stuck on a problem, do you often to think about it first, or act right away?

Q42. How easy is it for you to share your problems with your partner?

What aspects of yourself do you wish you worked on more?

Q43. How would you have utilized a Think Week as a grade school student?

A Think Week is a solo retreat to get away from the busy world, tend to your thoughts (or any books), and come up with solutions to any problems you may have. No meetings, no distractions. Bill Gates has been doing and preaching the importance of a Think Week for decades for its results in creative problem-solving.[5.3] A Think Week can undoubtedly help all of us tackle the third step in Dalio's five-step ambition process, determining the root cause of your barrier.

It is imperative to fully understand a problem before any form of solution can be made. Without the proper diagnosis of an issue, there are a million treatments that can go wrong.

In your past, how did you overcome barriers? You certainly would have had goals as a grade-schooler, regardless of how significant you think they were now. Think back to those days and place yourself back in those old shoes. Did you think you wouldn't make the school basketball team, the the saxophone solo, or pass that test? The way you diagnosed barriers back then is a strong indicator of how you currently handle obstacles. If you were given a full Think Week away from any obligations to solely research, think, and brainstorm your current issues, would you know how to diagnose them?

For You:

As you think back to your past, try to notice any patterns with your ability to understand your problems. The most common issue we face is our inability to distinguish between surface-level barriers and deep-rooted barriers: perceived causes and actual causes. This may sound like "I didn't make the team because I didn't get enough points" versus "I didn't make the team because I am not disciplined enough to practice."

You'll notice that surface-level barriers often use verbs ("because I didn't get enough points") whereas deep-rooted barriers use adjectives ("because I'm not disciplined").[5.1] Was this you as a young adult? Is this you now?

One method of getting to the heart of a dilemma is a frequently used technique called the Socratic method. In simple terms, the Socratic method requires you to ask "why" critically (at least five times) until you realize what the deep-rooted barrier you're facing is.

Why am I not making enough money?

Because my boss won't give me a raise.

Why can't I get a raise?

Because I'm doing all the work I possibly can and can't do more.

Why can't I do more?

Because I don't have enough time to spare.

Why don't I have enough time?

Because I need to plan my wedding.

Why do I need to plan my wedding?

Because it's important to me that it be perfect.

Why don't you trust anyone else to make it perfect?

Because I have trust issues.

In this critical dialogue, we can decipher whether problems lie within our control and how we can go about solving them.

For Your Partner:

Listen to the way your partner answers this question. How would they utilize a Think Week? Within the context of this section, guide their answer to stay on the topic of understanding their barriers and problems.

Remember, this is the time to think, not implement. This means the only thing your partner is really getting out of this Think Week is a strategy/plan for what to do once the Think Week is over. No doing. Just thinking. This will highlight how they go about defining their problems.

Maybe they're fantastic at strategizing, or maybe they're naïve to the importance of preplanning. Whatever way your partner tended to diagnose their problems in the past, it is your duty to help them now. Just like identifying any barriers, you must work together to fully understand the root cause of these barriers.

For You Both:

As a couple with goals, you must work as a team. Understanding your deep-rooted barriers to your goals is an imperative step to achieve them. Again, practice polite and open honesty with each other, as you both bring a unique perspective to your shared barriers.

Imagine you are both on a Think Week together—a pre-honeymoon, if you will. But instead of celebrating, you use this time to strategize your future together. To tackle any barriers between your current life situation and your dream destination. Coincidentally, marriage specialist John Gottman has found that this shared strategy and understanding of your goals is the number one principle to a lasting marriage. He calls it a love map.[5.4] Essentially, when you're on the same page with your goals and how you plan to conquer barriers, you are on the path to a stable and long-lasting marriage.

Follow-up Questions:

Q44. How much do you think you've grown at identifying the true causes of your problems?

Q45. Do you believe you would use a Think Week effectively today?

Q46. How often did you confuse surface-level barriers with deep-rooted barriers as grade-schooler? Do you think you are better at it today?

Q47. Use the Socratic method to determine a deep-rooted problem that you have about your wedding.

Q48. Design a seven-day schedule for a hypothetical Think Week to design your perfect wedding celebration (e.g. - Day 1 is determining budget; Day 2 is for researching venues; Day 3 is for researching vendors; Day 4 is for emailing out inquiries etc...)

Q49. Which of these methods of thinking were you most familiar with: divergent thinking or convergent thinking?

Throughout the mid-1900s, American psychologist J.P Guilford pioneered the paradigm of divergent thinking and convergent thinking.[5,6]

Convergent thinking is characterized by figuring out one possible solution to a problem (as opposed to multiple), utilizing well-established techniques to solve a problem, and determining specific and unambiguous solutions to a barrier. Most grade-school tests rewarded an individual's ability for convergent thinking.

Guilford found that individuals who tended towards convergent thinking conceptualize in black and white. Right or wrong. These individuals excelled in standardized tests with only one solution to a question, and they are often seen as book smart. Divergent thinkers, on the other hand, tended towards the grey area.

Divergent thinkers are flexible in their problem-solving and are less anxious about the "best possible answer." When designing a plan around certain obstacles, they brainstorm multiple potential solutions and know that there is no one-right-way to solve a problem. Guilford associated these individuals with creativity.

Think back to your grade school team projects. Which form of thinking did you tend to use? Do you use the same method of thinking today? Divergent thinkers often excel in a brain vomit, a brainstorming technique where all ideas are put on the table without holding back. Convergent thinkers often compare divergent thoughts with their true practicality, filtering them into refined solutions. Neither is better than the other and is often used together for the best problem-solving experience.

In this fourth stage of the "Five-Step Process to get what you want out of life", we are designing a plan around your barriers. For example, if you realize your budget does not accommodate your wedding needs, this is the step you design a plan to find the budget. Which method of thinking do you most associate with?

For You:

In your life, it is far more obvious to see the methods of convergent thinking being taught to you. As a student, you were tested on your convergent thinking abilities with questions that required specific answers, explanations, and black and white solutions. Perhaps you were routinely given outlines to write essays and concrete learning objectives for each subject you studied. Do you still let this method of thinking permeate into your current goals? Yes, maybe there was only one way to solve for x in grade seven, but you eventually learned different mathematical processes to do so. Do you allow yourself to experiment today?

For Your Partner:

Maybe your partner was, and always has been, highly creative. With an inclination to think outside the box, perhaps you noticed their patterns of creating new ways to conquer barriers. But maybe they're a little too outside-the-box and can't see the far stretch of their ideas.

Divergent thinking also has its pitfalls. Being too ambiguous or too open-ended to make practical sense. Sometimes, this faulty brainstorming arises from a lack of time management—remember, although you can achieve *anything*, you can't achieve *everything*. The limits of time and skill often make creative solutions unattainable within your situation. For example, you could solve a budgeting issue by starting and growing a new business for more funds, but can you really afford all that time and effort within the same timeframe as your wedding?

Probe your partner on their method of thinking. How would they design a plan around something in a realistic way? If it helps, go through a hypothetical problem right now. A common worry for brides and grooms is keeping on a timely schedule. How can you create a wedding day schedule that allows for all your required events of the day without needing to rush or be late? This is especially helpful for the camera, as feeling rushed doesn't help at all with flashing a genuine smile.

For You Both:

Together, complementary thinking is your best bet at creating a well-devised plan. Maybe one of you is inclined to think convergently and the other divergently. You both can come up with as many random ideas as you can and then filter it down to a focused and tight-knit plan.

If you both lean towards one method of thinking, it may be worthwhile to think oppositely. When you set out to make the basketball team as a grade-schooler or wanted the concert band solo on the saxophone, how did you set out to practice? Did you give yourself a set practicing schedule that you know works (convergent thinking), or did you research new methods of practicing (divergent thinking)?

As you and your partner approach your wedding day, maybe you're both stuck on making a feasible schedule. You've both tried to convergently follow the outline you found in your wedding-planning guidebook, and you've both tried divergent thinking to find better ways to fit everything in. If you've done everything you can together as a unit, there is no shame in asking for outside help. Professional wedding planners are a great investment in your sanity.

Follow-up Questions:

Q50. Which form of thinking do you tend towards while working on group projects?

Which of these methods of thinking were you most familiar with: divergent thinking or convergent thinking?

Q51. In your relationship, do you believe you take on the same or different methods of thinking?

Q52. Does traditional education keep you from solving problems by divergently thinking? Would you say you can think creatively?

Q53. Would you say you can smoothly transition into divergent thinking?

Q54. Go through your wedding day schedule (or a hypothetical wedding day schedule) and come up with a creative way to get in all the important events you want with at least 15 minutes of leeway time between them. Pro tip—treat driving to locations as an event.

Q55. When are you in flow state?

This is the last step in Dalio's "Five-Step Process to get what you want out of life". Once you've set your goals, identified any barriers, and devised the best plan you can around these barriers, all that's left is executing that well-defined plan. This can take the most amount of time or the shortest amount of time.

This step is your opportunity to execute a well thought out plan that can turn intention into action. While many good things can come from spontaneity, this is still a step that requires planning.

Carrying out your plans requires both skill and discipline. I've found that the best way to do this is by putting yourself into a flow state.

Flow state is being in the zone—being fully immersed, focused, and energized in the activity you are performing. Professor Csikszentmihalyi formulated this theory after interviewing dozens of experts from a variety of backgrounds, such as composers and chefs, to analyze their mental state and productivity. Flow is being in the *now,* this is when you are most present in the moment and don't get anxious, afraid, angry, depressed, or confused about anything else. People experience this state when they feel their bodies doing all the thinking for them. They've internalized the actions required to perform a skill and have a tunnel vision towards its completion.[5.5]

The most effective task-doers, those that can see their action plans into completion, are those that act in a flow state. As a grade-schooler, when do you think you were in a flow state? Do you still experience this state today? Determining the types of activities that bring you into a flow state will help you understand what types of tasks you are the best fit to complete.

For You:

When was the last time you lost yourself in a task? You most likely remember these flow states as enjoyable and fulfilling. Explain to your partner what kind of projects these are. Maybe it was that puzzle you put together or the jaw-dropping presentation you gave at your board meeting or baking two dozen cupcakes for your little sister's back sale. Whatever brings you to a flow state, explain these moments to your partner.

Do you notice any patterns?

Many psychologists define a state of flow requiring two main things: the performance of a skill that you enjoy (e.g. applying makeup) and a challenge that stretches your skill level (e.g. applying your own bridal make up in a short amount of time). When you can hone in on what your specialty is, it becomes easier to determine what tasks you should be implementing yourself. Just remember, it's okay to ask for help when the tasks you need to get done can be better accomplished with the support of someone else.

For Your Partner:

Help your partner see what types of tasks they are best fit to accomplish. Drawing on all our past experiences, you can probably define the types of skills your partner excels at. Maybe they can illustrate beautiful invitations or handle financial tasks with ease. Whatever you think they are good at, help them see their strengths by telling them.

On the other end, help them realize their weaknesses. We can't be good at everything. The successful completion of a plan hangs on the implementation. Maybe your partner lacks the skills, and you or someone else is better suited. If so, practice your affectionate communication and find a way to agree on a delegated honey-do list. Again, some things may be better suited for others to do. Wedding planners, wedding photographers, makeup artists, venue coordinators; they all have their specialty and are excellent sources of additional help to make your dream wedding come true.

For You Both:

Setting goals is an extremely thrilling activity to do with your partner, and it's just as fulfilling to work with your partner to achieve them. Remember, keeping a polite and honest atmosphere around these plans is imperative to your relationship and your ability to grow and master ambition.

Some things might require a better skillset and knowledge, and some things might require other people altogether. If you two are finding it challenging to complete a task, again, there is no shame in seeking more help. As you go through life's challenges, remember that you are both in this together—as a team of two individuals, a team of one unit, and a team that has friends to reach out to.

Follow-up Questions:

Q56. Do you still experience the same flow-state you did as a child? Is it better today?

Q57. What are you doing when you lose track of time?

Q58. Do you lose track of time doing similar things? Totally different things?

Q59. What tasks do you need to do, but also know that your partner would do them better?

Q60. If you had to do one job for the rest of your life, what would it be?

When are you in flow state?

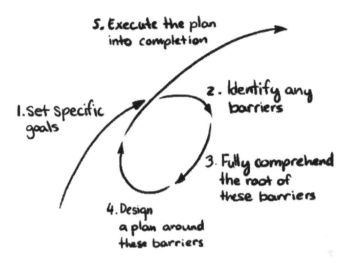

That's it! You've successfully gone through the steps you need to achieve personal growth and goals. The more you go through this cycle, the more aware you'll become of each step and what you need to work on.

Aside from these five steps, the most important thing to remember from this chapter is your teamwork. While you and your partner have been through a lot together, there's so much more to come. You are a team that needs to work together. Plan together. Act together.

As you fulfil your dreams together, there is no doubt that your relationship will become stronger. Take pride in your successes and your ambition, and let it show in the way you smile at one another.

STOP – Before moving forward:

How would you rate your element of ambition?

☐ 1 ☐ 2 ☐ 3 ☐ 4 ☐ 5 ☐ 6 ☐ 7 ☐ 8 ☐ 9 ☐ 10

How would you rate your partner's element of ambition?

☐ 1 ☐ 2 ☐ 3 ☐ 4 ☐ 5 ☐ 6 ☐ 7 ☐ 8 ☐ 9 ☐ 10

Rapid Action Steps:

1. Write down the number one area in your life that needs the most improvement with your element of ambition (e.g. goal-setting, strategizing, executing with your partner).

2. Every morning for the next week, wake up and tell yourself that you are going to act with better ambition in this area of your life. Let your partner know.

3. Read **The Power Couple's Playbook:**
https://aarondanielfilms.com/shop/the-power-couples-playbook

The Five A's

ARTISTRY

Wedding Day Confidence

6. ARTISTRY: Growing Expression

"One painter ought never to imitate the manner of any other; because in that case he cannot be called the child of nature, but the grandchild. It is always best to have recourse to nature, which is replete with such abundance of objects, than to the productions of other masters, who learnt everything from her."

- Leonardo Da Vinci

How to Define your Authenticity

After five years of shooting wedding films, everything changed for me.

From 2014 to 2019, my wedding work felt pretty much the same. Each film followed the same template, my shots of brides and grooms were all replicas, and my style of editing was nearly identical. I was stagnant.

Ask any creative mind to list their fears, and the idea of unoriginality will be there. Artistic minds need to keep learning and improving, especially if their livelihoods are on the line. For me, longing to grow was not just for my own sanity, but for the sake of every couple who expects their wedding film to be of high, modern standards.

Feeling ready for a change and aching for inspiration, I find out that two of my role models in the industry were about to host a wedding film course. It was not only perfect timing but the course's location, the beautiful province of Puglia, Italy, would set the scene for what would become a crucial learning experience. I booked my tickets and anticipated every moment leading up to meeting Remi Schouten of Maru Films (based in The Netherlands) and Riccardo Fasoli of Kreativ Wedding (based in Germany).

I lived in Italy for a week and took in as much of the country as I could. The wedding film course was only four days, but I came a few days earlier to soak in the foreign atmosphere. The unfamiliar food, the urban architecture, and the shopping centers are all things one can find inspiration in. I also got the chance to polish my Italian language skills and put a couple years of classes and self-teaching into use.

Once the film course began, I settled in with about fifteen other students. We each had a room in a quaint private villa. Picture a Mediterranean brick and stone building (a la bed and breakfast) surrounded with luscious plants and fruit-bearing trees enclosed by stone walls. Then add in a pool to take in the quiet starry nights, the perfect ending to a dreamy getaway. Any corner of the property would make for a beautiful fine art painting.

For our daily workshop coursework, we were seated in rows in front of a TV in the dining area. It was right next to the kitchen, where we would enjoy three meals a day together. Both Remi and Riccardo would present their lessons on the TV, along with showing their film editing process. Everything they taught me was so useful that now I find it hard to believe I did things any other way. From storytelling to business etiquette, filming, directing a couple on the property, and editing, we covered creating a beautiful wedding film from start to finish. It was an intense course that left me with unforgettable lessons and memories.

I often recall one lesson in particular. On the very first day of learning, Riccardo began his lecture on filmmaking with the following statement:

"You can be like a kebob shop, or a pizzeria, or a buffet, or a Korean BBQ restaurant."

Through his mix of an Italian and German accent, I didn't quite understand what he meant.

"Like food restaurants, you can create your films in many different ways. A kebob shop is usually very fast. A pizzeria only sells one type of food. A buffet has so many different foods. And Korean BBQ takes time to cook and taste," he continued.[6.1]

Riccardo would often laugh at his loss of words in the English language, so it wasn't uncommon to hear Remi chime in and clarify any ideas.

"One type of restaurant isn't better than the other. You just have to know which type you are making. Be authentic to who you are," added Remi.[6.2]

Authenticity. It turned out that the same characteristic that cultivates looking good on camera was also the one that enriches the filmmaker behind the camera.

"Improve your wedding films by being authentic. Find your voice."

The analogy of different restaurants to different types of wedding films is forever locked in my brain. The more I let the idea simmer in my head, the more I saw it trickling into the many different aspects of a wedding day. For instance, the way a wedding vendor helps piece together your wedding is often dependent on the type of weddings they like working. A fine art film photographer would likely often prefer to share their work of elegant décor, whereas a Parisian-style wedding florist may have a hard time designing decor for a rural barn wedding.

Your wedding is arguably the most personalized event in your life as a couple. The colour scheme, décor, venues, and vendors are often all handpicked. I challenge you to express your authentic voice as individuals and as a couple and let it shine through your celebration.

The type of work we create is defined by who we are as people, and that is exactly what this chapter is about: your element of artistry.

Whether you choose to believe this or not, there is a unique imaginative spirit inside you that longs to be understood. You came into the world with distinct genetics and have grown up with unique experiences, environments, and memories that are true to you. No one else on the planet can copy your taste with exact precision. You are, quite literally, 1 in 7.4 billion.

So, what does this uniqueness have to do with your relationship? I would say quite *a lot*, especially how you manage conflict in your relationship. Let me explain.

Conflict Resolution in a Stable Marriage

During early adulthood, we start to manifest our uniqueness for others to appreciate. We begin to see the ways our creativity can make an impact on the world. Working on company projects, dealing with customers and fellow coworkers, while infusing our expertise into everything. Consequently, this is also the time we begin to really take critique and criticism for our work. Up until this point, we were probably following in a mentor/professor/boss' direct footsteps, but early adulthood encourages us to put our creativity on the table. Open to be judged by those around us.

The way you take these professional judgements at work is the same way you take personal conflict at home, or at least it's very similar. When critiqued for your work presentation, how do you react? Most likely, you will fall under one of John Gottman's conflict resolution styles:

1. Validating
2. Avoidant
3. Volatile[6.3]

You may recall Gottman's 5:1 ratio of positive to negative emotions to create a stable marriage from Chapter Two. In his love lab, John Gottman has studied the interactions of hundreds of couples. Over the years, his research data has given us insight into helping countless relationships stay intact. Especially so with the following conflict resolution styles.

Validating Couples:

These are the couples that validate and reaffirm each other's opinions, even if they don't particularly agree with them. They are the poster example of emotionally stable couples, especially so with the traditional therapist.[6.3] Their mutual respect promotes openness for discussion and a sense of teamwork if a conflict arises.

The example below is the three-step sequence that validating couples go through whenever they encounter arguments:

1. Validate:

Partner A: I *really* don't like the décor options you picked.

Partner B: Oh? What is it in particular that you don't like?

Partner A: It's way too flowery and Pinterest-mom to me.

Partner B: Hmm.

Partner A: I know it matches the spring season of our wedding date, but it's just a little much.

Partner B: Well, it does fit in really nicely with the other décor. Our invitations even match the design and everything. It was really nice to have that checked off of our wedding to-do list.

Partner A: Yeah, that's true too.

Notice the openness for each other's opinions?

2. Persuade:

Partner A: But I do think we can turn down the florals down just a smidge, don't you think?

Partner B: [Laughs] Babe, you're overthinking it! I really think everyone will like it the way it is.

Partner A: [Also laughs] I know, I know, it does fit well with everything else. But I know it will be just as good or even better without so much… flower-power, you know?

Do you see how they try to persuade each other of their own opinions?

3. Compromise:

Partner B: Hmm, what would you suggest we do instead?

Partner A: I really do like the consistency of our décor and how it matches the table designs, invitations, and spring theme. But I was thinking we can limit the number of petals around the room. Petals and any décor that screams "this is a flower."

Partner B: Isn't that the main thing that makes it a spring-themed wedding?

Partner A: Not necessarily! Is that really the reason you want to keep the décor the way it is?

Partner B: Yeah, I guess so. You know me, consistency is key.

Partner A: But what if we replaced some flowers with something else? Something different, but still show the spring idea.

Partner B: Hmmm, well if you think there's a way to do that without dumbing down our strong design, I suppose it wouldn't hurt.

Partner A: Oh, I know my idea will work. Just let me try it and I'll show you how much better it will be.

Partner B: [Laughs] It better work, our entire marriage is on the line.

There is a sense of teamwork in this argument that is reminiscent of the way we deal with conflict internally with our element of ambition. We have our goals as individuals but work together as a team to make them come true. I do think these validating couples have the advantage of shared ambitiousness that makes their relationship blossom.

Volatile Couples:

Volatile couples are heavily engaged in their opposing opinions. When conflict arises, they dedicate a lot of energy trying to convince their partner of how right they are. Where the validating couples typically goes through three phases during an argument, the volatile couple skips the validation step and jumps straight to the persuasion and compromise phases.

1. Persuade:

Partner A: Babe, I really don't want you inviting this girl to our wedding.

Partner B: What the heck, but you were good friends at that party last year!

Partner A: Only because I know your group of friends are close to her. You barely talk to her unless you have to, and it doesn't help that everyone knows you had a crush on her before.

Partner B: Before! That was a long time ago and it doesn't even count. You know that. Besides, I know she really likes you, and all my friends think you'd be good friends.

Partner A: That still doesn't change the fact that you almost dated!

Notice how it went straight into rebuttals?

2. Compromise:

Partner B: Almost, but never did! We knew we weren't right for each other. That makes my relationship with you even stronger.

Partner A: That doesn't change the fact that you kissed her!

> Partner B: You've kissed other guys before me!
>
> Partner A: [Starts to laugh] Yup, and don't you forget it, mister!
>
> Partner B: [Joins in laughing] We invited that one guy who kissed you just weeks before we started dating. What's that supposed to mean?
>
> Partner A: It means nothing, he's coming with his fiancée!
>
> Partner B: Exactly! It means nothing, just like every other past relationship doesn't mean as much as our's right now.
>
> Partner A: I guess so…but it still doesn't change the fact that she could try kissing you again on our wedding night.
>
> Partner B: Babe, she wouldn't do that!
>
> Partner A: You never know!
>
> Partner B: Okay fine, since I know I'm just so irresistible [laughs again], what if we give her a plus one to bring with the rest of my friends? Would that make you feel better?
>
> Partner A: Hmm… you think she'd bring a date?
>
> Partner B: I'll have my friends make sure of it!
>
> Partner A: You'll just be too irresistible in that tux [laughs] okay fine… only because I know you're still friends. And only friends.

Although long and somewhat messy, the compromise still happens. Volatile couples, as loud or obnoxious as they can be in conflict, still give each other space to come to an agreement. They can be shouting and saying irrational things, but at the end of the day, they can make up for it by having five times more positive interactions than negative ones. Their arguments are just balanced out with more positivity.

Avoidant Couples:

The avoidant couple is the third and last of the stable marriage types. These are the duos that would prefer to minimize any thoughts of sparking conflict. Gottman says the more accurate name for these people would be "conflict minimizers" as they often don't see much benefit to bringing up issues with one another. They can agree to disagree and prefer to emphasize and focus on the positives in their relationship. This is their form of compromise. They completely bypass the first two stages of the validating couple sequence and only engage in compromising.

1. Compromise:

Partner A: Look at this beach resort, wouldn't it be fun to plan our honeymoon here instead?

Partner B: Hmm yes, but the prices look way out of budget.

Partner A: That's true, yeah, our country getaway still sounds good. I guess a beach isn't as important to me.

> Partner B: There's a lot we can do across the mountains and open skies.
>
> Partner A: Oh, and the beach might actually be a little harsh that season. I remember my sister saying it wasn't the greatest last year.
>
> Partner B: I know it would be nice to lay on an expensive beach, but we could use the money we save and put it towards the kitchen counter we were looking at. We're so close to finishing our renovation plans.
>
> Partner A: Yes, that would make so much more sense.
>
> Partner B: You wouldn't mind?
>
> Partner A: Oh no, no, we already have exciting plans that don't really need added expenses!

Do you see the retraction? Where the other relationships rely on engaging conversation, conflict avoiders tend to retract when there's a feeling of oncoming arguments. They'd much rather keep a stress-free relationship, even if it does mean sacrificing their personal needs and preferences.

The validating, volatile and avoidant couples are the precursors of a stable and long-lasting marriage. Within this chapter, we will look deeper into the sequences that these stable marriage types go through: validating, persuading, and compromising.

As you were going through the example conversations on the previous pages, you may have thought, "oh, this is totally me!" or "wow this is *so* my fiancée" or "dang it, I think I'm this one, but I want to be that other one."

Bear in mind that, just like the artistry within you, one style is not necessarily better than the other. Remember, it's all in the 5:1 ratio of positive to negative interactions. There are validating couples that break up sooner than extremely volatile couples and avoidant couples who outlast validating couples.

This chapter will help you gauge your style of conflict resolution and help make it easier to come up with an agreeable solution. We do this through the third element of The Five A's: Artistry.

Don't be fooled by the poetic title of this element, artistry is just our ability to create results with our work, either professionally or personally. The administrative assistant with a knack for organization. The respiratory therapist who understands her mechanical ventilation techniques. The retail stylist with an eye for aesthetic staging. It is the master of artistry who knows their place in the world and knows when and how to take criticism for their creative ideas and innovations.

When you are dealing with conflicting ideas about the work you produce, it is a signifier for the way you handle conflict in your relationship as well. Once you understand the way you best handle issues at work, you will better handle your relationship issues and promote positivity in our actions.

Are you ready to get to know your element of artistry?

Questions 61 - 90

ARTISTRY

Q61. How do you bring value in your profession?

Often, we perceive our value and self-worth in relation to the professional outputs we produce, and this is the consequence of living in a commercial-driven society. Generally speaking, the more value you bring to your employer or business is a measure that you may use to determine your self-worth. As a sales representative, your value increases with every sale you make. As a customer service clerk, you may see your value represented in customer reviews.

When we determine our self-worth in relation to company targets, sales, or whatever output is relevant to your line of work, there will undoubtedly come times when we feel unappreciated. What if your customer, boss, or co-worker doesn't see how much your experience, creation, or ideas are worth? Value contradictions arise, and this can spark conflict.

For example, a community worker registers a few participants in a support program to create an intimate and comfortable experience. Their supervisor, stressed by project targets, might emphasize the importance of registering a higher number of participants. Or a media content producer spends three weeks writing a long feature about a topic they're passionate about, but their editor is demanding more frequent and shorter clickbait pieces.

These are points of contention that could lead to an erosion of self-worth, and even conflict. The same idea can be applied to personal relationships. For example, one partner thinks a frugal budget is most important and emphasizes saving money, but another partner values experiences and would much rather spend their dime on restaurants and vacations.

This question aims to help you understand what *you* value most about yourself and your work. You may realize that your values are in line with your work, or perhaps you experience cognitive dissonance; when your behaviour, attitude, and beliefs conflict with one another. You may come to various realizations when answering this question, but what's most important is that you develop a clear understanding of values that are most important to you so that you can effectively communicate it.

For You:

Miscommunication is one of the most common sources of conflict. Having a clear idea of your stance is the first step to communicating effectively and avoiding misunderstandings. Take a moment to think about your answer, and then help your partner understand where you place value. Think about potential alignments and misalignments in value systems and share those too.

While this question is intended to be answered within the context of your professional life, societal, cultural, and environmental factors would inevitably influence your answer. Think back to when you first started in your line of work: what types of values did you like to promote? Help your partner see the values you like seeing and embodying in your line of work.

For Your Partner:

Don't take this question for granted because you may think you understand your partner's values already. Values are not stagnant in time; they change as we change. It's also important to know your partner's values in their line of work, not just the values they hold within the context of your relationship and family life. As you grow more together, you and your partner's work lives will become much more intertwined than you may believe. If you don't understand the work-related values your partner sees, you leave yourself vulnerable to misunderstanding what's important to them, which can lead to conflict.

Probe your partner on their work ethic and what they appreciate in their professional life. If they are the type that finds pleasure in client reviews over sales made, you may see them emphasizing experience over money. If they appreciate making money over saving, you may see them tending to take more risks financially. Look for these trends in their answer and see how you can relate it to what you know of them already.

For You Both:

The goal of this question is to get you and your partner to understand values in relation to work. Having a shared vision or at least a known vision of what you value will help you develop a deeper connection and avoid conflict.

When you know where you each stand, where you like to show and appreciate value, you begin to act with empathy for each other's wants and needs. This ultimately creates a space for positive interaction.

If, however, you do need to bring up your opposing thoughts, let's find out if you are the first type of couple in a stable marriage in the next pages.

Follow-up Questions:

Q62. On a scale of 1 to 10, how much do you believe your professional colleagues understand your worth?

Q63. What topics tend to make you the most argumentative in your relationship?

Q64. Why is your job special to you?

Q65. What do you appreciate the most about your profession?

Q66. Which values around work do you and your partner share the most?

How do you bring value in your profession?

Q67. Why do you think your coworkers like talking to you?

Let's face it; we like people who are like us.

Have you noticed that you tend to purchase from vendors who share your similar values? Maybe when you were shopping for a wedding planner, florist, or officiant, there was something about them that said, "hire me, I'm just like you."

Am I right? Now think about your coworkers or fellow industry workers. Which ones do you like hanging out with or talking to? Probably the ones that are like you! The ones that validate your personality because they share a similar one.

Now think about how friendly you are in your work relationships. Of the people who openly speak to you on a friendly level, why do you think they like talking to you? Obviously, they must like you and share some sort of similar characteristics. Does this include your openness and ability to validate other opinions or ideas? Recall that validating is the first part of the conflict-resolution sequence and is only seen in the validating type of couple. The goal of this question is to see if you are the type that thrives in a validating relationship.

Do you believe coworkers like speaking with you for your input on their ideas or simply for the amusement you bring them? Do you think you create time and space for them to speak their mind, or, now that you think of it, you are more likely to strong-arm your own opinions? This question is meant to help you determine how validating you are.

For You:

Yes, the people you work with might like talking to you for a number of reasons, but as you begin to share your answer with your partner, you will start to notice a pattern indicative of the type of relationship interactions you lean towards.

Someone who leans towards an avoidant conflict resolution style may respond to this question with: "I agree with everything they say," "I'm just so laid back," or "I'm good at highlighting the silver lining."

If a volatile relationship is more their style, they may respond with: "I just have all the answers," "I'm way cooler than the others," or "I do everything better."

A response that resonates with a validating relationship interaction would sound like: "I listen deeply," "I encourage their ideas," or "I help them elaborate."

Can you see the resemblance between your interactions with your colleagues at work and your partner at home?

For Your Partner:

Maybe your partner thinks their coworkers like them for their talent, or work ethic, or even their looks. Probe deeper than this. Where the last question spoke of their professional value, this question takes a step back and looks more at their personal value. Their ability to connect on an emotional level. Are they validating?

Get them to paint a picture of their professional interactions, and then ask about the personal feelings they get when speaking. Do they emit a sense of highly-engaged volatile behaviour or conflict-avoiding reactions?

Remember, their actions could change depending on the person they envision speaking to, so ask them about multiple people. Their boss, coworkers, customers, and clients. Why do these different types of people like interacting with them? There will be a pattern among all of them, though at varying scales. Do you see a strong ability to validate others?

For You Both:

Determining your affinity for validating each other is an important step in conflict resolution. Whether you have a strong affinity towards it or not, practicing validation in your relationship can only bring good.

Perhaps each of you leans towards different types of interaction, and that's okay, but you do have to meet each other using an approach that feels comfortable to both of you. That will allow for quicker and smoother problem-solving.

How much importance do you place on feeling heard, accepted, and acknowledged? If this is of utmost importance to you, then your relationship should work towards incorporating validating behaviour.

If perhaps validation does not resonate with you *and* your partner, then your relationship likely falls into the other types of stable marriage interactions. Which we will explore with the next pages in this chapter.

Follow-up Questions:

Q68. Who are the work friends you enjoy being around? Why?

Q69. On a scale of 1 to 10, how open are you to listening to their ideas?

Q70. When do you most validate your coworkers' ideas? When are you least validating?

Q71. How intimidating do you think you are around your colleagues?

Q72. Who are three people you speak differently to? Explain why.

Why do you think your coworkers like talking to you?

Q73. Describe who you look up to in your industry.

The art of persuasion relies on your engagement. How engaged are you in sharing your personal opinions, proving you're right? If you believe you do have validating tendencies, this is the second step in conflict resolution. If, however, you don't think validating is important, persuasion is where the volatile relationship types start their conflict resolution.

This is where your role-model comes in. The person you look up to in your industry. This is also the person you most likely want to show off to your family. Why? Because you believe in the work they do and who they are, and that is presumably who you want to be like.

To a high degree, our role-models in our field of work are the people we subconsciously emulate. When we see their art, we try our hand at their style. When we see their communication style, we try to mimic their tone. When we see their taste in music, maybe we try listening to their playlists. Our role-models are doing something we aspire to do, and we want to be on a similar path.

Now, this is where the fun comes in. When you think of this person, how would you describe them? How you do this, your level of engagement and enthusiasm when vouching for them, is synonymous with how you persuade others of your ideas. In a sense, your role-model is your idea of excellence, and it is this very idea that you're trying to persuade other people of. Now, what happens if others don't subscribe to your idea?

For You:

Who are the icons in your industry? Who do you come back to again and again for inspiration?

Be as open and honest as you can. Imagine you and your partner were at a work party; you're nibbling away on the supply of hors d'oeuvres when all of a sudden, your role-model comes up to you. You know who they are, but your partner is oblivious. You exchange brief introductions, and this person parts ways, but not without giving you their contact. Before they walk away, they ask you to reach out to them within the week to work on a project together. Inside your head, you are over the moon. As soon as you leave the party with your partner, you can't stop raving about how incredible it was to meet this person! Your partner is clueless. How do you explain this person to your partner?

For Your Partner:

We all have our idols in our line of work. However, sometimes these idols aren't necessarily a common topic of conversation at home. You might be completely oblivious to the people your partner looks up to, just like they might be about your role-models. This is your chance to get to know who they look up to, but most importantly, the purpose of this exercise is to see how they try to persuade you into liking this role-model as well.

A role-model is a reflection of our goals and ideas of who we want to become. When your partner explains who this person is, you can assume this to be a reflection of your partner's ideals.

Listen to the way they speak about this idol. How strongly do they feel about who they are and what they do? Is your partner engaging? Next, subtly try to disagree with them. How defensive or volatile do they seem to get? The way your partner will impart their opinion here would likely resonate with their approach to conveying their opinions in general.

For You Both:

Let this play out. How much energy do you put into persuading or disagreeing with one another? Your role-model may be the best in the world, but your partner might not see it that way. How invested are you in this opinion? How invested are you in your other opinions?

After discussing the person you look up to, try speaking about other people in your industry. The discussion can shift to talking about the people you most dislike in your field and the reasons why you don't like them. Describing the way you both like and dislike someone is an easy first step into understanding the way you defend your opinions. Do you notice any patterns? How much energy do you put in? Again, this is an indicator of how you likely persuade in other forms of conflict.

Now that you're attuned to your persuasive techniques and tendencies, we can move to our next stage in conflict resolution.

Follow-up Questions:

Q74. On a scale of 1 to 10, how engaged are you at trying to persuade your coworkers?

Q75. Do you believe you persuade your significant other drastically different than your coworkers?

Q76. What do you think your partner will appreciate most about your role model? Least?

Q77. How defensive would you get if your partner disagreed with your role-model?

Q78. Who is someone you dislike in your industry? Explain why.

Describe who you look up to in your industry.

Q79. On a scale of 1 to 10, how assertive do you think you are?

Compromise is essential to all our relationships, whether they are with our colleagues, friends, family, or partner. How assertive do you think you are in this process?

Generally, high levels of assertiveness are indicative of volatile behaviour, mid-high levels are more in line with validating behaviour, and low levels are a sign of avoidant behaviour. In the previous questions, your answers illustrated your tendency towards the validating and volatile relationship types. Now, we will look into the avoidant style.

Avoidant couples almost always compromise as their first (and last) line of defence in conflict. They skip validation and persuasion and go right into agreeing with each other's wants. Recall that they would much rather keep to the very positive aspects of their relationship than to place heavy emphasis and energy into addressing any disagreements. Conflict is hardly given time and attention. However, avoidant relationship types, much like the avoidant attachment style described in Chapter Four, has its downsides as well.

When you show a low ability of assertiveness, this can lead to feelings of seclusion or emptiness. You risk losing passion. If there weren't any other distinguishingly positive interactions, there wouldn't be much spark in your relationship. How assertive do you feel you are?

In your workplace, how often do you fight for your opinions and ideas? Are you known for going over-the-top in proposing new projects, or do you retract at the first word of disagreement? How avoidant do you think you are, and how sacrificing are you when compromising?

For You:

Paint a picture for your partner. During your last team meeting or last interaction with a client, how often did you find yourself keeping your thoughts to yourself?

Maybe you had a lightbulb moment around a team problem but thought it would be too extravagant to be accepted? Or perhaps you were excited to share your ideas with a client, only to find out they decided to work with someone else, so you didn't say anything.

Again, different environments provoke different reactions in you, but you will notice trends. Sacrificing your immediate wants in favour of a bigger positivity is something I see in a lot of couples, especially during a hectic schedule. For example, during a busy wedding day, you and your partner might sacrifice taking a nap, enjoying hors d'oeuvres, or going to an alternate photo location so that everything stays on schedule.

How forgiving are you of conflicting needs? And how much do you fight for yours?

For Your Partner:

Maybe you know for a fact that your partner is absolutely stubborn and would do anything to get their way. They are the extraverted speaker in your relationship and speak with a powerful voice for what they believe in. In this case, it is safe to assume that they would not fall into the avoidant type of stable relationship. However, it is still just as important to understand the way they handle compromises.

From one to ten, the scale of assertiveness gives you a good idea of how you deal with arguments together. As with all our questions, speaking directly about your relationship might lead to biased answers, so we keep the topic about work. How does your partner mend any professional arguments?

For You Both:

The first step in compromising is understanding where both of you stand on the spectrum of negotiation, i.e. how assertive are you both? Being on the same level helps you both keep eye to eye, where one doesn't overpower the other too much. This alignment in action is your anchor in conflict. Like a seesaw, if there is too much energy on one side, the imbalance will lead to even more conflict in a vicious circle of negativity. If your dynamic isn't balanced, you might find yourselves saying, "I don't think you see it my way," "I value your agreement over being correct," or "I don't understand you, so I must be right."

A balanced seesaw will keep you in a choreographed trance, always sharing the same energy and motives towards a mutual agreement. This is the goal. Not too sacrificial and not too greedy. Ideally, you will both want the same things, but when opposing opinions do collide, you can engage in a shared level of compromise that promotes smooth solutions. Remember this during future arguments. Keep a balanced level of energy, and conflicts will naturally take its course as smoothly as possible.

Follow-up Questions:

Q80. How often do you fight for your ideas in the workplace?

Q81. Would your colleagues describe you more of going over-the-top in proposing new projects, or someone who retracts at the first word of disagreement?

Q82. When do you tend to sacrifice your initial ideas?

Q83. Describe a recent argument that caused you to compromise a lot.

Q84. True or false: you tend to fight to be right before mutual agreement.

On a scale of 1 to 10, how assertive do you think you are?

Q85. When do you feel the most accomplished and fulfilled?

The three types of stable relationships handle conflict very differently. Validating couples start by validating each other, volatile couples start by persuading each other into their own beliefs, and avoidant couples start by compromising their needs. By now, you've hopefully determined which of these three types of styles resonates with you and your relationship.

This last question takes us beyond these three styles and focuses on your reaction and acceptance of compromising. When do you feel the most accomplished and fulfilled in the workplace?

We all have those times where we agree just for the sake of agreeing. We complete unwanted tasks and projects just because we have to, not necessarily because they bring us joy, pleasure, or a sense of self-worth. Your answer should not focus on these but rather help you and your partner understand what types of compromises you *like* making. Your best accomplishments rely on you coming to a resolution, solution, or goal that fits your joint life missions.

For You:

Your answer should emphasize big moments at work that spark a sense of fulfilment and accomplishment in your actions. Your product. Your creation. Your art. Your salesmanship. Whatever it is, let your partner know.

The goal of this question is to share your true inner desires. To see what types of solutions you like to emphasize and want to bring into the world. If your partner's wants conflict with your ideas, you both will have a hard time letting go of these ideas. But if your partner knows what matters to you, what really brings you a sense of accomplishment, then it is more likely your partner will be open to your thoughts.

If it wasn't something that you *really* wanted or ignites a sense of passion, then it wouldn't affect you as much anyway.

For Your Partner:

Take note of your partner's accomplishments at work. What are the things that they like to bask in, and what gives them joy? You might have an idea of these things right now, but probe as deep as you can. This question will not only provide you with insight into what they like doing at work but can also help you see where your arguments could get drawn out too far. For example, if they enjoy experimenting at work, then maybe they like to play around with furniture layout or colour schemes, and this gives them a sense of joy. Or perhaps they feel most accomplished when they close a big sale after months of waiting, and this translates into them patiently planning out their new furniture design instead of rushing into it because they enjoy moments of delayed gratification. Look for the patterns in what makes them feel accomplished at work and how it can translate to your relationship.

For You Both:

This question comes back to you seeing eye-to-eye. You both need to be on the same level to move forward together. Even though the types of tasks that bring you a sense of accomplishment might be different for you and your partner, you need to recognize, acknowledge, and respect your differences. If you don't, then you may risk hindering or diminishing each other's accomplishments. And that can only lead to disappointment and resentment.

Follow-up Questions:

Q86. Do you believe you have a validating, volatile, or avoidant conflict resolution style with your partner?

Q87. How often do you dwell on arguments you've had to compromise on?

Q88. What ethics are you absolutely not willing to compromise on in your work life?

Q89. When do you feel the most passion for your line of work?

Q90. Which highly-rewarding tasks at work do you believe you can do for your relationship as well? (E.g. organizing schedules, reading finances, décor choice).

By now, you've likely noticed patterns in each other's needs, behaviours, and personalities that are relevant across each of The Five A's we've previously discussed. Your element of ambition brings your goals to fruition, and your elements of affection and artistry allow you both to support one another along the way.

The first three elements of The Five A's are the fundamental trifecta of a fulfilling relationship. Through learning more about each of these elements and examining their corresponding life stages (early childhood, school years, and work-life), you've developed a deeper understanding of yourself as an individual and as a unit in a relationship.

These phases of our lives are the building blocks for who we set out to become. Once we've established a career, we generally have two options: to continue living within the confines of that career path or to grow and learn outside of it. Next, we will discuss how the elements of awareness and awakening shape the rest of your life and your relationship.

STOP – Before moving forward:

How would you rate your element of artistry?

☐ 1 ☐ 2 ☐ 3 ☐ 4 ☐ 5 ☐ 6 ☐ 7 ☐ 8 ☐ 9 ☐ 10

How would you rate your partner's element of artistry?

☐ 1 ☐ 2 ☐ 3 ☐ 4 ☐ 5 ☐ 6 ☐ 7 ☐ 8 ☐ 9 ☐ 10

Rapid Action Steps:

1. Write down the number one area in your life that needs the most improvement with your element of artistry (e.g. - validating, persuading, compromising).

2. Every morning for the next week, wake up and tell yourself that you are going to act with better artistry during conflict in this area of your life. Let your partner know.

3. Follow my personal artistry on Instagram:
https://www.instagram.com/aarondanielfilms

ARTISTRY

The Five A's

AWARENESS

Wedding Day Confidence

7. AWARENESS: Expanding World

"The world is becoming ever more complex, and people fail to realize just how ignorant they are of what's going on. Consequently some who know next to nothing about meteorology or biology nevertheless propose policies regarding climate change and genetically modified crops, while others hold extremely strong views about what should be done in Iraq or Ukraine without being able to locate these countries on a map. People rarely appreciate their ignorance, because they lock themselves inside an echo chamber of like-minded friends and self-confirming newsfeeds, where their beliefs are constantly reinforced and seldom challenged."

– YUVAL NOAH HARARI

Do you remember when you first met each other?

What was that like?

A new world of opportunities. Thoughts of shared holidays and vacations, maybe? Or finally, a dinner date you could bring to all your friends' weddings and parties.

When couples inquire about my work, I ask them how they met and to describe their proposal to me. I often receive wholesome responses like: "we were in the same physics lab together, and we've been inseparable since," "we knew each other since we were toddlers but slowly got closer as adults," or "we worked on the same office floor and started going to all the same work events together."

These replies help me understand their relationship dynamic, but I also think it gives these brides and grooms time to reflect on how much they've grown with their spouse-to-be.

When you ask your married friends how they met, I'm sure there will be some form of spark in their eye. From the couples I've asked, there will always be one meet-cute story that I frequently tell my friends and often think back to again and again. The reason it's so shareable and relatable is that it gets at the heart of the origin of all married life: being prepared.

Being prepared enough to not only ask a life-changing question but to also take on a wholehearted dedication to another person.

Being Prepared

I was with Megan and Joe at a Starbucks and we were just about to wrap up our meeting.

We went through their entire wedding day schedule and what specific shots they would want in their wedding film. Then it got more personal. They explained how and *why* they met and the reason their meet-cute was so meaningful.

"You find her when you stop looking and when you least expect it," explained Megan. I smiled in wholehearted agreement. Joe, however, offered more to this sentiment.

"Yes, that'll probably happen… but just like most other successful happenings in life, you'll be prepared for it. Like the same way you do well at work or in business. You'll be internally prepared as an individual. I thought I was always somewhat prepared to be in a relationship, but it wasn't until I knew 100% that I was ready that I finally met her," added Joe.

"I don't want to turn this into an esoteric answer, but it happens when you're genuinely confident, as an individual, to be in a relationship. A definite relationship you know you want. So, yes, I agree with Megan that you may not be explicitly looking when you find your partner, but you would have already been mentally, physically, and financially ready for it when it happens."

In other words, you're more likely to find your partner when you're not looking, but only because you are, and you have been, focused on being prepared to be in a place to welcome this partner into your life.

And I believe the same holds true for weddings. Being able to have a wedding doesn't just rely on preparation for a day of festivities but being prepared for a lifetime of marriage. Your steady and stable marriage is a by-product of your preparedness and continual growth together. How prepared do you think you are to move forward?

After this meeting with Megan and Joe, I started noticing preparation being a key aspect of many couples taking their next steps into marriage–in ways you may not expect.

Christine and Arslan:

Christine's family is from The Philippines, and Arslan's from Pakistan. Although their wedding did not show any favour towards one culture or the other, it was fantastic to see their traditions coming together. Christine and her bridesmaids wore Tikka, glistening Pakistani headpiece jewelry. These cultural pieces were new to her family. Arslan, on the other hand, was being introduced to some Filipino dancing music during the reception. I can only imagine the planning of this wedding, including conversation about their traditional expectations. These early conversations are their form of preparation, being prepared for the unfamiliar.

Kassandra and Peter:

Kassandra is Polish, while Peter had a Serbian and Greek upbringing. These cultures have unique wedding traditions, and the couple fused different customs to throw an unforgettable wedding celebration. They also made sure that each of the families were aware of the activities that would take place. For Peter's family, this meant partaking in a humorous gesture of "bribing" the bride's family with money, alcohol, food, and even animals on their doorstep. Imagine a driveway party with folklore music, dancing, and lots of food. The guests enjoyed making an entertaining ruckus as they waited for Kassandra to come out of the house in her wedding dress. Later that night, the couple ceremoniously shared some bread and salt, a common Polish tradition, to symbolize a lack of hunger and being able to cope with life's struggles. Kassandra and Peter's wedding was probably one of the most enjoyable films I've made. It would not have been the same if I didn't anticipate these events beforehand. And I'm sure Kassandra, Peter, and their families would have been confused if they weren't filled in on the meaning behind each of these traditions.

Milana and Srdjan:

Milana practiced a vegan lifestyle for years, and around the time of their wedding, Srdjan started getting into it as well. I'm sure it took a fair bit of effort to practice a vegan lifestyle, but they've done it together. About two and a half years after their wedding, they both started filming vegan recipes and posting them on YouTube. Over time, their channel, Plant Lana, grew into a space where they can share and experiment with vegan recipes with other foodies on the internet. Would they have been able to do something like this without their shared expertise? Probably not at the same level. Without taking the time to understand the vegan niche, which we can describe as a form of culture, they wouldn't have been prepared to create a channel that is beginning to rack up thousands of views at the time of writing this book.

Weddings and married life can come with surprises. In these stories, individuals and families learned from rituals that were new to them. You might have some ideas about how you want to celebrate, but you both might not be on the same page. This chapter intends to get you and your partner on the same page about traditions you might not be aware of or have paid little attention to before.

Specifically, this chapter will help you better understand your culture and your partner's. Not only to ease the process of planning your wedding but to support you in the greater scheme of human understanding. You are preparing to take on the world and experience the beauty of our diverse cultures together. How aware are you?

The element of awareness is your ability to relate to others. In other words, your willingness to meeting your partner's needs which are rooted in cultural expectations and values.

Meta-Programming:

What we know about the world influences the way we interact with it. In turn, interactions become engrained in our mind, informing our approach to new encounters. Meta-programs, which are mental shortcuts that direct decisions, behaviours, actions, and interactions with others, describe this phenomenon.[7.1] Essentially, meta, which means over and above, indicate that there are programs in our mind that interpret the world and the way we react and make decisions.

In this chapter, we will look at how you and your partner interpret the world around you. As the luxury sales coach and author of *Sell with Style,* Carlo Pignataro, explains, "Meta-programs are, in a certain sense, the 'operating system' for the human mind. They are the mental patterns that allow all of us to process experiences and that, to a certain extent, 'program' us to interact in a particular way. They affect how we absorb information, interact with others and react to experiences."[7.2]

Pignataro has worked in sales and marketing positions for luxury companies like Gucci and has consulted for Giorgio Armani and Gianni Bulgari. He knows a thing or two about global luxury markets. Having briefly exchanged emails with him, it was his ideas about high-end servicing that defined the way I should be servicing those around me and how everyone should be treating others: by actively listening to one another.

Society to society, our cultural assumptions have evolved and grown in our ever-shrinking world. Cultivation of our element of awareness is necessary for successful cooperation between people, and most importantly, cooperation between you and your partner.

This chapter will look deeper at five questions within the context of meta-programming. Questions will explore your general knowledge of our world's many cultures and your expertise in a specific culture. We then determine your cultural biases when making important decisions, which will help you and your partner better understand why you do the things you do.

These areas of discussion will give you a blueprint for each other's subconscious meta-programming. And as exemplified in the stories of Megan and Joe, Christine and Arslan, Kassandra and Peter, and Milana and Srdjan, meta-programs help us anticipate how our partners interact with us. If you say *this*, they will say *that*. If you do *this*, they will do *that*. When *x* happens, you can assume *y* will happen. I learned about this while working with couples of new cultures, but this also works wonderfully in my relationship with my girlfriend's Polish family traditions. When she does x, it helps me understand her feelings of y, leading me to act with z.

Throughout this chapter, you'll notice that the questions aren't exclusively about you and your partner as a couple. The questions invite an understanding of all humans. As you and your partner will learn, the element of awareness is imprinted on us every time we meet new people. Specifically, when we travel or interact with an unfamiliar culture. We can read and watch as much as we want about other traditions, but it is in the act of engaging with these different communities that bring us the most education. When we immerse ourselves in the daily lives of a new culture, we become part of a new world of opportunities and beauty.

For you and your partner, how well you can connect is seen in the way you know the rest of the world as well. Where did your partner grow up, and what was it like? Where did your partner's parents or grandparents grow up, and how has it affected their upbringing? The more you can experience the world, the easier it becomes to empathize and connect on a deeper level with your partner.

And like all our other chapters, we will use a specific stage in your life as a proxy for how you do things now. This life stage, the established career phase, is likely the stage you're in at the moment. It is described as the point in your life when you're feeling relatively settled, both professionally and personally.

Up until this point, the elements of affection, ambition, and artistry have influenced you. Now, it's time to sharpen your awareness. You have a steady means of providing for yourself and have new capabilities to explore the world. As I write this, most of the world is transitioning into a new pandemic reality. While many are experiencing lockdowns, various justice movements around the globe are demanding our awareness (and action) to imagine and create a future that is free of oppression. I encourage you when answering the questions in this chapter to think about your place in your community and collective efforts for justice and peace in all relationships.

This chapter's questions prompt you to think about your understanding of the world and what role it plays in your relationship. They are meant to spark a deeper understanding between you and your partner, effectively making it easier to bring out positivity. Your internal theatre will continue to build its reel of positive emotions together and ultimately help you two smile. So, let's sharpen your element of awareness in each other, examine your thoughts on the world, and bring our meta-programming to light.

Questions 91 - 120

AWARENESS

Q91. If you could reimagine your birth, what would it look like?

Culture is our means of differentiating ourselves *and* relating to others. The reason some cultures lose their prominence and some seem almost universal is due to the influence of the group that practices it. We can look to music as an example; some genres of music start as very distinct or even niche, and over time they become accepted as popular music. Rock and Roll started with generational hate in the '50s, but Elvis and The Beatles helped pave its way into the mainstream. Mongolian yodelling, as wonderful as it may be, just doesn't have the same traction today. The reason for this is the amount of influence that the respective authorities have on the world. The purpose of this question is to develop an understanding of what types of cultures have influenced you the most and where your general knowledge lies.

While birth is a universal occurrence, the environment in which you are born into can lead to an infinite amount of possibilities. This question, like all our questions, is open-ended to allow you to dig deep and be imaginative. If you had the choice, what would your birth look like? Is it in a hospital or at home? What national, economic, or political environment would you have wanted to be raised in? With this question, I invite you to speak about how you would have liked things to be different (or the same).

With everything you know about the different places in the world and their different customs, traditions, and political realities, how would you have chosen to be born?

For You:

This question is open-ended and invites you to synthesize all the knowledge you have. You could have been born into a royal family. You could have been born in a Mediterranean village. You could have been born as your parents were travelling in Tibet. You could have been born with none or all of your relatives near you. Why would you want this?

Don't hold back, and don't try to be too realistic. Allow yourself to explore the unimagined, and sink yourself into an almost dream-like world that you are creating for yourself based on what you know of current realities. For example, wanting to be born into a political family with your parents, each originating from warring countries, all for you to bring peace between those two countries. Another example could be claiming the fortunes as the heir to an industry mogul. Or it could be something as simple as being born into a quiet little town just a short distance from the peaceful ocean coast. Explain to your partner why you would want things to happen a certain way.

For Your Partner:

Dig deep into your partner's reasoning, and don't be afraid to guide them in different directions. There isn't a right or wrong answer or a genuine response we can take from this hypothetical question. Guide them, and don't be afraid to offer your suggestions based on what you think they'd want. You can remind them of something they would have wanted to say or introduce something new to them. In this way, you can help them be more aware of the possibilities out there.

Feel free to ask them creative guiding questions:
- What about having Santa Claus as a dad?
- Wouldn't you prefer a family who travels for a living?
- How about being born with siblings who had superpowers?

The possibilities with your partner are endless. Our imaginations are only limited by the ideas we think are out there. Your partner's answer shows you where their imaginative limits are, with you as someone who can take them further.

Awareness in your partner is ever-changing, and this question can be a fun one to ask every-so-often with new insights. One day they may think one way of being born would be perfect, then the next day, they learn something new and change their answer entirely.

For You Both:

I challenge you to hold this question everywhere you go. When you first answer it, be mindful of your current mindset and perspective on how the world works. Your understanding of the economy, politics, and media influence can change in a heartbeat, and the way you wish you were born might not be so perfect anymore. Your perspective can and should change as you learn more from the world.

Remember, the underlying meaning behind reimagining the way you were born is to share your general cultural knowledge of the world. How you answer this question shows your unique understanding. Your partner should challenge that knowledge and help you explore realities beyond the borders that are familiar to you. Every second, four people are born into the world, and each birth is unique.

Follow-up Questions:

Q92. Who do you think has the most influence in the world today?

Q93. On a scale of 1 to 10, how strongly would you have wished to be raised differently?

Q94. Why do you think your birth into the world was perfect for you?

Q95. Why do you think your birth into the world was completely wrong for you?

Q96. Do you actively stay up to date with general world knowledge?

If you could reimagine your birth, what would it look like?

Q97. Where in the world do you think you best fit in?

We can't change the environment we were born into, but what we can do is change the environment we are currently in. There are a million things to see and do, and that's just in your home town. The world is at your fingertips, quite literally with your phone. With a click of a button, you can search, see, and engage with people and places around the globe. The internet is a place of connection and discovery. Of all the types of people and places you know of, where do you think you'd best fit in today? Explain why.

This question touches on your current interests and is an opportunity for you to share what's most important to you. This question aims to build on little pieces of cultural trivia to reveal where your expertise lies. Remember, culture encompasses the ways social groups make life meaningful through languages, customs, beliefs, food, arts, and knowledge. There are many different types of cultures, such as hip hop culture, startup culture, football culture. For example, you might be informed and interested in technology businesses, and places like Silicon Valley or Berlin could be where you imagine yourself fitting it. Or perhaps you see yourself in Venice, Italy, because of your expertise in theatre, opera, and Italian food, which you believe comes together perfectly in this city.

For You:

Out of all of the places you've been to or learned about, there's likely a particular spot that stands out to you. You may have already thought of this place while growing up. Perhaps it was a family cruise to Jamaica, a friend's wedding in Santorini, or an Instagrammer's trip to the coast of Melbourne that has left you with a positive impression. Whatever it was, you just had to Google it. You found out what was there, and you fell in love with what your life could be like if you lived there. Share this place with your partner.

Again, this is a free-for-all answer that could go in many directions. You could perhaps think of it with an emphasis on your career, raising a family, or retiring. In these cases, list all the places you would eventually like to be part of and make sure to explain why.

Remember, this is just a gateway question to showing your partner what you believe is important. Where you believe you fit in is also the place where you believe all your needs will be met. If it meets one of your needs but not another, then this isn't your answer, you'll need to think harder. Determine a place that feeds your elements of affection, ambition, artistry, and awareness. Brainstorm and share your thoughts with your partner.

For Your Partner:

Guide your partner. This question might need a lot of brainstorming. You may have visited this place with your partner already. A small mountain village in Poland, a town full of hikers along the Rocky Mountains, or a busy metropolis in Thailand. Which of your travels sparked the most engagement with your partner? Remind them of these moments.

The way your partner answers will give you an idea of what they value most and where they put a lot of their energy. For example, the hiking town could have been where your partner can indulge in their hobbies as a botanist, or that busy city in Thailand could be the best spot to open a new branch for the global fashion magazine they work at.

Maybe you didn't expect your partner's answer. Perhaps you didn't know they have a knack for speed reading or an affinity for HTML coding. This question can reveal areas of expertise and interest you may not have been aware of before.

For You Both:

Remember that this question will help you understand each other and yourself on a deeper level. As you both come to understand where you like to be, it becomes easier to understand yourselves as a couple. Your expertise in cultural knowledge helps highlight what's important to you as individuals in the world and can prompt a plan to help make you feel like you're in the place you best fit in.

For example, if you answered Manila, Philippines as the place you best fit in because of its relation to your family and vicinity to the ocean, we can gauge that these things are most important and known by you. Your partner can use these reasons (i.e. a tight-knit family and the closeness of the relaxing ocean coast) to help ease stress as you encounter it. They can bring up that your family is just a phone call away and plan a tropical vacation to look forward to together.

The following process is a starting point to relieving any stress or conflict:

1. Location X is where you best fit in because of reasons Y
2. Reasons Y can be found or related to things in your day-to-day lives
3. Highlight how reasons Y can be felt or achieved in your current situation to ease stress and encourage happiness

Use this process as much as you need and make a game out of this question as often as you'd like!

Follow-up Questions:

Q98. How do you typically lose track of time while surfing the internet?

Q99. What cultural phenomenon are you currently interested in?

Q100. List your top three dream places to live in.

Q101. Which of your travels sparked the most engagement in you and your partner?

Q102. Complete this sentence: "I feel accepted where I am now because…"

Q103. When planning a trip, do you fill your schedule or do you leave it open?

While it may seem that we get stuck in our familiar ways of thinking, it is possible to change our meta-programs for the better. To do so, you have to bring awareness to the meta-program and choose to change perspective. This question intends to explore your meta-program for making decisions: do you either look for external proof or do you rely on your intuition?

There will be times in your married life when you encounter difficult decisions that you and your partner can't seem to agree on. You will rely on methods of conflict resolution that are most comfortable for you (as referred to in our previous chapter), and your meta-program for decision-making will kick in.

This meta-program, looking for external proof versus internal intuition, may orient you towards persuading your partner on what you think the decision should be. Through persuasion, you are sharing proofs and reasons to back up your stance. But how you develop these ideas depends on, again, your meta-program: do you look for outside evidence or rely on your intuition?

Pignataro notes that people who rely on external proof look to others for guidance and acceptance.[7.2] The feeling of fitting in is a big motivator in how they decide to make decisions. This means that if you sway to external proof, you may make decisions based on other's opinions and how it influences your image in front of others. This doesn't necessarily downgrade your independence; it just shows that you would prefer a bigger consensus for acceptance. For example, you may choose to post selfies on Instagram with well-known clothing brands, thus feeling like you fit in.

On the other end, those who rely on their intuition are very proud of who they are as individuals. They know they can do things on their own, and they make their independence known to those around them. For instance, sharing selfies on Instagram with clothing brands that *aren't* well-known, thus showing their distinct independence. In Pignataro's experience, these individuals tend to buy items that showcase their uniqueness.[7.2] They don't need as much assurance from others.

Those who act with internal intuition are very much like the avoidant individuals we learned about in our chapter on affection. And those who act with external proof are much like the anxious individual. They either prefer a lot of validation or a lot of independence. Which one do you think you are?

For You:

If you've already concluded you have an anxious or avoidant attachment style, you can be fairly certain that your meta-programs are influenced by either an external proof or intuition. Just remember that neither is better than the other and are simply ways of quickly understanding how you might make biased decisions.

For example, when we look at this question, would you fill your trip schedule, or would you leave it open? Those who fill their trip schedules tend to be very confident in the way they make decisions, whereas those with a completely open schedule are open to what others bring their way. Which schedule would you choose?

Depending on what you tell your partner, you can begin to see how this meta-program guides you. Understanding your meta-program will help you understand your biases when you make future decisions. And this will keep you both accountable in your decision-making processes.

For Your Partner:

You likely have the upper hand when answering this question. It can be more difficult for your partner to answer this question, whereas you can piece together their tendencies from a more objective point of view. So do you think your partner would prefer to pack your honeymoon full of to-do lists or leave it completely open to being swayed by the winds?

In terms of their meta-program, this question helps you anticipate the bias in their decisions. Do they tend to rely on others for approval or take pride in their independence? Once you gauge which way they lean, catch them when they lean too far. Remember that you are a team, and if you catch them making unreasonable decisions, remind them that it's their meta-program that might be stopping them from seeing the bigger picture.

You could literally say:

"Honey, I think you are looking for too much external proof," or

"Honey, I think you are relying too much on your own biased intuition."

For You Both:

Maybe you're deciding on your honeymoon trip, or your ceremony venue, or the number of groomsmen and bridesmaids you wish to have. Whatever decisions you're making, think back to this meta-program and how your independence or external validation may be the biggest obstacle to making your right move.

Keep in mind that there is no right or wrong answer to being influenced by others or by listening to yourself. The most you can do when making these decisions is by having an open discussion with your life partner and coming into agreement.

Follow-up Questions:

Q104. Do you act based on external proof or your own intuition?

Q105. What motivates you to buy certain foods?

Q106. Describe a recent moment you let this meta-program influence you into making a regrettable decision.

Q107. Do you think you are easily influenced?

Q108. When was the last time you completely disagreed with your partner? Was this due to one of you having an external proof meta-program while the other used their own intuition?

Q109. When in all of history, other than right now, would you have liked to live?

This question touches on another meta-program: your tendency to either relieve pain or gain pleasure. When making decisions, you are either looking to move away from discomfort or move toward joy.[7.2]

Depending on the situation, this motivation can change.

Think back to the last time you had to make a big decision. What were your reasons for making your decision? Were they fear-based or pleasure-based? This question intends to help you determine how likely you sway to either side.

Choosing a time in history does multiple things for your understanding of each other. On the surface level, you learn even more about each other's awareness (e.g. showing how much you know about a country's history, a city's political changes, or a province's educational infrastructure). On a deeper level, you gain insight into your partner's motives: are they running from pain or looking for pleasure? When in all of history, other than right now, would you have liked to live? Explain why to your partner.

For You:

History has its many ups and downs, and sharing your knowledge of these historical moments helps your partner understand just how knowledgeable you are. Not to mention, you never know when this trivia would come in handy.

As you share your answer with your partner, fully detailing your reasoning behind your chosen time in history, you begin to show your meta-program for decision making. Do you tend to look for solutions that relieve pain or gain pleasure?

When in all of history, other than right now, would you have liked to live?

For example, you may say you wish to live in the 1960s. There are many reasons you might want this. Watching The Beatles play live could be your motivation and source of pleasure. Or you could be looking to run away from today's politically charged internet, which is relieving pain (though the '60s could arguably be just as heated in other ways). Perhaps you wish to live in medieval times. Your motivation could be to live the devoted life of a well-regarded knight, or perhaps you just want to put on a suit of armour and joust with others all day to relieve stress. A third, less eccentric, example is choosing to live in feudal Japan. Either for gaining the pleasure of becoming a samurai or relieving the pain of today's office-culture that makes a rice farmer's life a beautiful idea.

These are all specific examples, so try to be as detailed with your answer. You'll notice that you can agree with both sides of reason, both relieving pain and gaining pleasure, but for this question, try to emphasize one reason and the things that matter most to you.

To help, list your top five reasons for wanting a one-way time travel ticket. What is your number one reason for taking that trip?

For Your Partner:

What is your partner's reasoning for living in a different timeline?

If history isn't something they are too familiar with, help them explore an answer. Bring up topics from history class or period movies. Exposure to history can be from all sorts of sources like comic books or musical lyrics. You can even spend some time researching together.

Maybe your partner can't put their finger on a specific moment in time. That's fine! If you need to, allow them to fill in the blanks with things they assume would be happening. Remember, the point of this question is to gauge their pain vs pleasure motivations.

It might help to get started if you get them to complete this sentence:

"I want to live during a time where I can…"

For You Both:

Did you find a time to live, and did you write that list of five reasons down? When you look at the list, are the majority of the reasons in favour of relieving pain or gaining pleasure? Maybe it was just barely a tie, in which case try to give more reasons or try to emphasize one side or the other. Don't overthink your choices too hard.

Once you understand which is your default motive, you can help each other catch your biases. Exactly like our last question, understanding your meta-programming helps you highlight where you might be unnecessarily favouring one option over another while in an argument. For example, if you're stressed about taking a long time with family photos and would rather be at the reception hall, would you rather be eating to feed your hunger (relieving pain) or talking to specific guests you haven't seen in a while (gain pleasure). If you understand these biases, it becomes easier for you both to make the right decision. Just remember, you want to give your cameramen enough time to work with you ;)

Follow-up Questions:

Q110. Was your last big purchase made out of fear or out of pleasure?

Q111. Do you believe you make more decisions to relieve pain or to gain pleasure?

Q112. List your top five reasons for wanting a one-way time travel ticket.

Q113. Complete this sentence: "I want to live during a time where I can…"

Q114. When thinking of your wedding schedule, what times do you believe will cause the most pain? What will cause the most pleasure?

When in all of history, other than right now, would you have liked to live?

Q115. Why do you, or why don't you, feel connected enough in the world?

Lastly, we will be looking at the meta-program that highlights similarities and differences. Pignataro describes this as the matcher vs mismatcher personality trait.[7.2] In terms of customer service, buyers are hard-wired to either look for the match in items or highlighting the differences. Matchers look for things that spark a union or a sense of togetherness with those they have in mind (e.g. speaking with strangers at a party and finding your similar interests in water polo). Mismatchers dwell on the differences (e.g. having conversations at that same party about how much you dislike the other person's favourite sport). In the context of your relationship, I'm sure you can already see where this can pop up.

When you and your partner are in a stressful situation and need to get something done, your tendency to match or mismatch can sway how you accomplish something. Your problem-solving is influenced by being a matcher or a mismatcher. For example, when you are on the hunt for a wedding videographer, photographer, DJ, or florist, the endless choices can make this task challenging. When you meet with these wedding vendors, the way they speak to you can trigger either your matcher or mismatcher interpretations. A matcher might be thrilled that their DJ shares the same music preference as them, whereas a mismatcher would notice all the disliked music in the DJ's library.

Likewise, when your partner is giving you reasons to hire one photographer over another, the matcher inside you might agree with all their reasoning. The mismatcher in you might look for all the faults in your partner's reasons. Each of these cases is equally valid, but it is up to you as a couple and as an individual to find a mutually beneficial agreement.

This question helps you determine if you are a matcher or a mismatcher. Why do you, or why don't you, feel connected enough in the world?

For You:

Gaining introspection on how you feel, or don't feel, connected to the world is a gateway into your matching vs mismatching self. In a nutshell, do you notice how similar or dissimilar you are?

Subconsciously, this question gives you the ability to share your deeper meta-program with your partner. If you say yes to feeling connected enough in the world, you sway towards the matcher (the majority of people). If you say no to feeling connected enough, then you sway towards the mismatcher. Explain why you feel this way to your partner.

For example, your explanation may sound like, "I feel connected enough in the world because I feel like I can talk to many people about many things. However, I know many of my close friends and family have a hard time starting a conversation."

The reason this is such an important concept to share is that, again, it allows you and your partner to be aware of how you behave in different situations. For example, feeling similar can lead to a sense of security around most people, while feeling too different requires specific people and specific situations to help them feel comfortable. Open up to your partner about how comfortable and connected you feel with others.

For Your Partner:

As with all our other questions in this chapter, your partner is giving you insight into their biases. This meta-program helps you identify how they interpret the world, either seeing similarities or differences in things.

If your partner *does* feel connected enough in the world, perhaps they are comfortable with the many different people in the world. If they *don't* feel connected, perhaps they only have a specific group of people they feel comfortable around. Ask them probing questions to get a more comprehensive answer. This will help you in the future to make decisions based on how open they are to new situations or familiar situations.

To bring back our DJ example, if they want to hire a DJ because they share similar tastes in music (acknowledging similarities), but the DJ doesn't fit your wedding budget (acknowledging differences), make this known to your partner. Guide your partner into making the right decisions for you as a team. Granted, no one ever has the perfect answer, but two heads are better than one, especially when they're in love.

For You Both:

The matcher and mismatcher meta-program is a concept so powerful in understanding human nature.

A prime example of trying to persuade your mismatching partner could go something like this:

> Partner A: "Oh honey, I'm not sure you'd really like this new barbecue sauce. I don't think you'd like it."
>
> Partner B (mismatcher): "No, no, it's something interesting, we should try it!"

Little did Partner B know that Partner A already planned a surprise gift with this barbecue sauce.

An example of persuading a matcher:

> Partner A: "Yes babe, this florist has all the nicest designs, we NEED her for our wedding!"
>
> Partner B (matcher): "Oh wow yes I agree! Look at all those flowery things, let's book her!"

Partner B had no idea about the florist's true talent and was just inclined to stay on the same page with Partner A.

Use this meta-program to your advantage as you take on the world together. Remember that you two are a team that needs to filter what you see. Don't succumb to any negative influences. You have each other's support, and with these meta-programs giving you a blueprint for your inner thoughts, you can help each other see where your faults may lie and how to get out of discomfort.

Follow-up Questions:

Q116. Do you mostly notice how similar you are, or do you notice how dissimilar you are around others?

Q117. On a scale of 1 to 10, how comfortable do you feel around the people you spend the most time with as a couple?

Q118. What groups of people do you feel the most connected with?

Q119. How often do you make decisions based on how different they are?

Q120. In what situations do you like seeing similarities, and what situations do you like seeing differences?

Throughout this chapter, you learned about your general cultural knowledge, biased expertise, internal vs external frames of reference, relieving pain vs gaining pleasure and seeking similarities or differences. With an understanding of your element of awareness and relevant meta-programs, you and your partner are prepared to discover a world of possibilities together.

Knowledge and experiences of the vast cultures and ideas of the world can help you as a growing family. Take in what you learn and apply it to your mutual benefit. How do you learn these new things? What do you want to learn more about? How do your meta-programs influence the way you interact with the world? Always keep these questions in mind.

Maybe you're just starting to travel more often or perhaps you've seen a lot of the world already. Whatever the case, sharing your experiences, knowledge, and perspectives is the first step in helping each other find positivity. Remember, being on the same page with your internal theatre helps make it a positive theatre. Allow yourself to smile as you watch the world.

In the next chapter, you will learn to smile not by looking out, but by reflecting in.

STOP – Before moving forward:

How would you rate your element of awareness?

☐ ☐ ☐ ☐ ☐ ☐ ☐ ☐ ☐ ☐
1 2 3 4 5 6 7 8 9 10

How would you rate your partner's element of awareness?

☐ ☐ ☐ ☐ ☐ ☐ ☐ ☐ ☐ ☐
1 2 3 4 5 6 7 8 9 10

Rapid Action Steps:

1. Write down the number one area in your life that needs the most improvement with your element of awareness (e.g. - addressing a specific meta-programs).

2. Every morning for the next week, wake up and tell yourself that you are going to act with better awareness.

3. Read 10 Books Every Power Couple Needs To Read:
https://aarondanielfilms.com/blog/10-books-every-power-couple-needs-to-read

The Five A's

AWAKENING

Wedding Day Confidence

8. AWAKENING:
Inner World

> *"Once there is a certain degree of Presence, of still and alert attention in human beings' perceptions, they can sense the divine life essence, the one indwelling consciousness or spirit in every creature, every life-form, recognize it as one with their own essence and so love it as themselves. Until this happens, however, most humans see only the outer forms, unaware of the inner essence, just as they are unaware of their own essence and identify only with their own physical and psychological form."*
>
> *- ECKHART TOLLE*

"I'm ready to sue," I kept hearing in my head.

There was a gnawing pain in my stomach. It flipped upside down, and I was ready to barf. An interviewee was threatening to sue over quotes published in a newspaper article I had written, claiming he never gave his approval.

I retraced my steps. I was profiling the individual about his life and work. I had asked for consent before the interview, received a verbal agreement from the interviewee on tape, and all the quotes were audio recorded. Confused and nervous, I asked the editor-in-chief if there were any grounds for a lawsuit. He assured me I didn't have anything to worry about, I was just doing my job, and this situation wasn't uncommon in the industry.

Still, I felt undeniable guilt. Had I known that this interviewee's word choice might reflect poorly on him, I would not have published the interview.

Either way, I had to suck it up. Guilt and embarrassment have funny ways of gnawing at your state of mind. I was trying to act like everything was alright, but on the inside, I felt a need to repent indefinitely. This feeling is incredibly hard to keep down as I made my way out of work and to a big meeting.

I was on my way to Coffee Culture in Stoney Creek, a café where I love meeting couples. This time, however, I was there without my usual dose of excitement. My order of their delicious turkey club came with a side of guilt, and the couple noticed.

Sarah and Adam had their wedding about three months prior, and I had the pleasure of filming it. I was hand-delivering their wedding film package, a particularly joyous occasion for me. However, the idea of being sued just kept my mood a bit salty.

It's always wonderful catching up with newlyweds. Sarah and Adam had been house-hunting and keeping up with some new work. As tough as it is to take on the challenges of marriage, these two were handling it with strength. You can see the ambition in the way they made new ends meet, their strong affection for each other, the artistry in the work that they do, and the awareness for each other and their family's needs. I'd say family is an important value to them, and the respect they show for those close to them is something to admire.

After about half an hour of catching up and telling them to wait until they get home to open their wedding film package, they asked how I was doing. They asked me about the busy wedding season, how cool it is to live a travelling cameraman's life, and my work at the newspaper. I didn't know what to say about the last part. I stuttered, not wanting to mention the potential of being sued, and told them that I was currently dealing with some issues at work.

They both looked at me with heartfelt eyes. Adam, in his gentle and sympathetic voice, broke it down to me in this way:

"Hey man, do what you gotta do, but don't let it get to you. You don't have to tell us any details, but don't stress yourself over this.

It's like the five by five by five rule my mom used to say to me. Will it matter to you in five days? Will it matter to you in five weeks? Will it matter to you in five years? If not, don't let it bother you."

I let that sink in.

Five days? Maybe.

Five weeks? Unlikely.

Five years? Not at all.

He was right. Thinking that far ahead, I knew that I could always find a way to keep myself on my feet after a potential lawsuit. The worst possible scenario would not, in fact, matter in five years. If I get sued (which was highly unlikely), there's a chance I could lose my full-time job, a job that I only planned to be in for less than five years.

A few minutes later, we wished each other good luck and went our separate ways. I let the five by five by five rule sink in even more.

"Will it really matter to me?"

WILL IT MATTER IN 5 DAYS?

WILL IT MATTER IN 5 WEEKS?

WILL IT MATTER IN 5 YEARS?

I was feeling a little better about myself after hearing this. I knew I didn't do anything wrong at work, and I had no reason to be worried. It just so happened that the very next day would be the perfect getaway from any remaining guilt.

I took the five by five by five rule from Adam and kept it in my thoughts as I went into the long weekend. I was headed to my friend Daniel's family cottage for the Civic Holiday up in Ontario's cottage country. Daniel had invited a group of our university friends to stay the weekend. As nervous as I was about coming back to work the following Tuesday, this cottage retreat was the perfect break.

During some quiet downtime between dock-side drinks and sausage grilling, I brought Daniel aside and asked him what was going on at work. He also worked with the newspaper team, handling the finances of the publication. I brought up what was bothering me and asked what he thought I should do about potentially being sued.

"Huh, what?! Oh, dude, you don't need to worry about that. There's no way you did anything wrong."

It was a relief to hear him consoling me. As fratty as this cottage getaway sounds, it calmed me down, especially at night.

I started to think about all the positive blessings in my life. One of my closest friends was hosting a getaway vacation on the lake, Sarah and Adam just reassured me of my value as a wedding filmmaker, and the group of friends around me were all letting loose with a drink or two. I finally gave myself some slack and stopped worrying.

I stopped worrying so much that I started dancing to a song by Florida Georgia Line between some rounds of flip cup. One of my friends recorded it on my phone, and without giving it much thought, I posted it on my Instagram story. Sure, the beer may have helped me calm my nerves, but it was that five by five by five rule that helped me put any worries into perspective. I was finally having fun, and I wanted to show it!

Then a few minutes later, someone replied to that Instagram story of my dancing.

"You're my fave 🖤" is what she said.

I didn't know her at the time, but the girl who replied was a guest at a formal event I filmed a few months prior. We followed each other on Instagram after briefly meeting at the event, thinking maybe she'll contact me when she needs a wedding videographer.

She didn't need a wedding videographer, at least not on this night.

I asked Daniel and the rest of the cottage gang if they knew her, and no one did. So, I kept the conversation going with her through Instagram.

From what I remember, we both had a few sips of alcohol that long weekend night and kept our Instagram DM conversation going. An hour or two later, we moved to text messaging. Then a few hours after that, we moved from talking about the music we dance to, to the places we'd like to visit. Then we got into the types of weddings I like filming, and what we would want for our own weddings. By this time, it was three in the morning, and I was not nervous about a lacklustre sue threat.

By six a.m., we fell asleep, but the conversation never ended.

That's how Amanda and I started talking and eventually dating. I credit it to the five by five by five rule, the release of any worry, and the simple act of enjoying myself with others. If I had kept an uptight attitude, who knows if I would have dared to post that embarrassing video of my dancing. Who knows if I would have been dancing in the first place? And who knows if I would have been open enough to continue that all-night conversation? Whatever the case, I hope all couples can practice this in their day to day lives.

Living In The Moment

Every wedding has its moments of worry. Are the flowers all set? Will the limo be on time? How is my hair? Should I try to pee now? At one point or another during your wedding, these questions will cross your mind. However, you should be spending the day enjoying it, not worrying about it.

As Eckhart Tolle says, release the pain body. This unhappy entity feeds on negativity, like the anxiousness of your future or your past's negative memories. To let go of this pain body, you must live in the moment and stop overthinking.[8.1] The element of awakening, the last of The Five A's, will help you in doing so.

Your element of awakening is your ability to let go of overly anxious (future-based) or depressive (past-based) thoughts. Inspired by Tolle's book, *A New Earth: Awakening to Your Life's Purpose*, this fifth element brings all of The Five A's together. It is the guiding star that brings your elements into balance.

Awakening can be thought of as letting go, going with the flow, egoless-ness, presence, entering the tao. As woo-woo as this might sound, awakening is your ability to focus on only the present moment. It is coming into, as Eckhart Tolle teaches, the power of now.[8.2]

Whether or not you're familiar with Tolle's teachings, or other forms of spiritual guidance, I'm going to use this final chapter to teach you the premise of understanding your element of awakening. Although most teachers in this field speak to the individual, I will help you and your partner build upon your shared skills of this element. Awakening as a couple is one of the highest forms of intimacy, and I believe it so important to your wedding day experience. When you two can relentlessly live in the moment, your wedding day will be the most unforgettable event of your life.

This chapter helps you identify if you're stuck living in the past or caught up in living for the future. We will also explore how you experience the present. While we explored the first three elements by looking at your childhood and adolescence, and the fourth element encompassed your present experience, the fifth element is ever-present in your life. Awakening has, and will always be, the guiding light in your world.

There is no particular time in your life that your element of awakening grows. Some couples sharpen this element during childhood, and some might be hearing about it for the first time now. When did you first come into contact with practicing presence?

Whether you are familiar with this concept, there will always be a chance to be more present and to forgive and let go. That is why, for this chapter, we will look at all stages of your life.

Are you ready?

Wedding Day Confidence

Questions 121 - 150

AWAKENING

Q121. Describe an embarrassing moment that still makes you shiver.

You're going about your day, maybe putting away some groceries, and then all of a sudden you remember *that* embarrassing moment. You forgot someone's name. You tripped over a rock. You said a joke that didn't land. It doesn't matter how severe the actual moment was, it's the sheer idea of doing something embarrassing that makes you shiver. When these embarrassing moments happen, we can do one of two things: feel awkward for a second, or let it haunt us for the rest of our life.

It's the haunting that changes who we are. This question aims to get a sense of your attachment to these haunting moments. Some events in our lives can have long-lasting impacts that we may never forget, but it's the way we deal with these events that determine who we are.

When we live too much in the past, we may start to take on feelings of hopelessness, loss, and emptiness. Your memories may influence your feelings, thoughts, and behaviours, and this can impact your mental health, wellbeing and relationship. And as I'm sure you know by now, this also shows on camera.

How prone are you to getting caught up in the past? Describe an embarrassing moment that still makes you shiver.

For You:

As you describe an embarrassing moment from your past, really paint that moment for your partner. Describe in detail what happened and how it made you feel. You may start squirming as you do this. My face is scrunched up right now just thinking of my embarrassing moments. The goal here is to let your partner in on these trivial embarrassments and air out some hidden pain. In addition to squirming, you both may start laughing. This is good.

Keep your partner laughing or consoling you, and soon you will allow yourself to smile and accept it too. I know this may sound weird as you describe it, but the more we can laugh or talk about our faults, the easier it becomes to accept them. You may have noticed this happening as you've gone through this book!

After you've described this past moment, begin to think about it as if it were happening in the future. I want you to imagine something just as embarrassing happening sometime soon. It doesn't have to be your wedding day, but maybe the day after or a few weeks later as you get back into the swing of your daily lives. Describe this event as if it was happening in the future. It could be a presentation at work, or catching up with friends, or your first holiday event as a married individual. Then invite your partner to be there during this moment.

For Your Partner:

Put yourself in the moment with them. As your partner describes this future act of embarrassment, describe what you would be doing as if you were right beside them. It doesn't have to be realistic. Pretend you're somehow at this hypothetical presentation, meeting or family event.

Now, after listening to your partner describe this future embarrassment, tell them what you would do. Show them that you'd be able to laugh it off with them, or sympathize with them, or help them. And at the end of it all, you both (and whoever else is near you) start to laugh it off as well.

You accept that it happened.

For You Both:

Let it play out. And let yourselves reassure each other that everything is okay.

The great thing about this little scenario is that it never actually happened. This hypothetical moment of cringe-ness might happen, but you also saw that it turned out just fine in the end. Your ability to predict this outcome is so much more enhanced as you begin to master all our other elements of The Five A's, namely awareness and just how attuned you are to other people's thoughts and actions. You begin to see that your little mistakes in life don't matter in the long run.

In your relationship, I want you to remember this: momentary pain doesn't have to last. You don't have to let moments of annoyance, irritation, or anger get to you. I know wedding parties tend to let their hangry-ness get to them (myself included), but you can tell a person's character by the way they keep calm during these times.

Life is meant to be enjoyed.

Follow-up Questions:

Q122. What types of memories embarrass you the most?

Q123. How often do you believe to be in a depressive state?

Q124. Describe an embarrassing moment that makes you laugh.

Q125. Predict and describe a future embarrassing moment that includes your partner.

Q126. What do you tend to think to yourself when you feel embarrassed?

Describe an embarrassing moment that still makes you shiver.

Q127. What upcoming event are you most frightened of?

High-risk moments are often the most fearful. When we know something important is on the horizon, our fear starts to overtake us. Hearts begin beating faster, the fight-flight-freeze response starts to kick in with adrenaline, and the mind can only think about what this future moment will hold.

Will I blow the meeting? Will I forget something? Will I come off as too strong or too weak? Will I forget to bring the rings? What if I mispronounce my speech? When do I say "I do" again?!

Just like the last question, the way you deal with these internal fears defines your character. You can either hide from it and react impulsively to whatever happens (which mostly leads to stumbling around), or you can emotionally prepare for it with as little as a few minutes of thought. What upcoming event are you most frightened of?

For You:

Think about doing something that you know could be difficult. Usually, this is something that you don't experience often. It could be meeting up with wedding vendors, having a rehearsal dinner, saying a toast, or having all your family over to celebrate. Whatever it is, describe this event to your partner.

After describing the scenario, explain why it frightens you. What part of this upcoming event leads to fear or anxiety? Illustrate as clearly as you can. Who's there, what are they doing, and what are you doing? What are you afraid of happening?

Finally, list the outcomes if your fears did play out.

For example, some people are afraid of giving speeches. In the wedding world, this looks like parents, brides, grooms, and wedding party members trembling a bit just before they introduce themselves on the microphone. During the wedding day mornings, I often see them writing and re-writing their speech, trying to memorize it or improve it. Some people are afraid of messing up or embarrassing themselves in front of their guests. One piece of advice I often share with nervous wedding parties is to remember *why* they're giving a speech.

The greatest antidote for fear is reminding yourself why you're putting yourself through it in the first place. This taps into your element of ambition and helps you understand the ultimate goal. Envisioning the goal helps put fear into proper perspective.

Once you share some of the outcomes of your (realistic) worst-case scenarios, start to list the best-case scenarios.

For Your Partner:

Help your partner list down the outcomes from the best-case scenarios. For example, that speech you give could spark inspiration for many others who are about to get married. It could bring happy tears to everyone's eyes, and serve as a reminder of how important it is to love. The entire room could start treating the rest of the world with kindness.

Another example could be the benefit of pitching an idea to your boss. The presentation you give might scare you, but the upsides are limitless. You could start a whole new way of working, a new product or service that leads your company down a significant path to grow.

Maybe it's starting and promoting that new business idea your partner had going through their minds. Maybe they're embarrassed to start something new, but there is so much opportunity in bringing this new opportunity, this new artistry, into the world. Starting a tutoring business could ignite the fire in future world leaders. Starting a sustainable makeup brand could help big companies downsize their environmental footprint.

Starting an Etsy shop for other brides to purchase your wedding designs or floral décor could make it easier for brides all over the country. Whatever fears are present, there is an infinite amount of opportunity waiting to turn into gold.

For You Both:

Once you list out the (realistic) worst-case scenarios and as many best-case scenarios as you can think of, you both will begin to see just how important this upcoming event truly is. Sure, there may be fear or anxious emotions while thinking about it, but as you start replacing these frightening thoughts with opportunistic ones, it becomes easier to prepare for them.

It becomes more exciting for you both to take on challenges.

So, whenever you two start to feel anxious about something, remember why you're doing it in the first place, list the worst-case scenarios, and list the unlimited number of upsides. This approach will give you the mindset necessary to keep you going.

Follow-up Questions:

Q128. Describe doing something you know would be difficult for you to do.

Q129. What are the worst (realistic) consequences that could happen?

Q130. Remind yourself and your partner why you are going through this in the first place?

Q131. What are the best-case scenarios that could happen because of this happening?

Q132. What makes you excited for your future with your partner?

What upcoming event are you most frightened of?

Q133. What upcoming event are you most excited for?

Now, let's look at an upcoming event that is already bringing you excitement. On a surface level, this question will help you share what is important and fun to you. It could be a promotion at work, a long weekend getaway to the cottage, or landing new clients.

Keep in mind, however, that when you talk about your optimism for the future, you are not only sharing your hopes and dreams but also shedding light on what you might feel you lack in the present moment.

For example, you're excited to move into your new home. Aside from a few more papers left to sign, your plans are all set to settle into a beautiful, two-floor townhome. While excitedly thinking about how you will own a home for the first time, you realize this future event will give you a sense of stability and prosperity that you lacked previously.

For You:

Think deeply about something you are excited to do. What is it that will excite you the most? If this event is your wedding, why is it something you're excited about?

The party?

The friends and family?

The vows?

The official documentation of marriage?

The food?

For Your Partner:

Help your partner describe this upcoming event. Ask them for details to determine their reasoning behind their excitement by asking "why?" as much as you need to.

For You Both:

You may choose to explore the feelings of excitement about your honeymoon. This celebration is worth the enthusiasm, but an exaggerated excitement can make everything else happening seem incomparable and unworthy.

When we look forward to something with *too* much excitement, we may develop tunnel vision. This can make it seem like nothing else matters as much. This may lead you to feel unappreciative of what is currently around you at the present moment.

While excitement is a wonderful feeling, don't let a fixation on future events take away from appreciating what you currently have. Solely focusing on the future is akin to dangling a carrot in front of a horse. It can create an endless chase.

When answering the question, you can use the following format:

Partner A: I think that _____ will be exciting because _____.

Partner B: And why would that make it more important than what we have now?

As a couple, make sure you take the time to talk about your optimistic future together and the growth of your relationship. You should also regularly discuss all the things you are thankful for. As important as it is to be hopeful, I believe it imperative to be just as happy for what you currently have.

This is especially important when you approach your wedding day. So many things are changing around you as you begin to move into this next stage of life. With everything up in the air, the unknown can be a stressful yet exciting time.

I want you to remind each other that right now is all you can be sure of, and it is something you should both be grateful for. The future can be exciting, but it is only your present moment that is promised.

Follow-up Questions:

Q134. What do you feel like you lack the most in your life?

Q135. What excites you the most for your upcoming wedding?

Q136. Describe a past excitement that caused you to only think about that event all the time.

Q137. Do you believe you are too distracted when you think of upcoming exciting events?

Q138. What are you most thankful for right now?

What upcoming event are you most excited for?

Q139. Describe a recent compliment you received that boosted your self-confidence.

Self-confidence is attractive. It is a characteristic that is universally appreciated. Many of us have grown up to idolize and trust self-assured people, and many of us aspire to attain confidence. Self-confidence may have helped you muster the courage to propose a new project at work, start a new business, or even pop the question.

Some people lack self-confidence and have little trust in themselves, while others know how to harness their self-confidence to achieve what they want in life.

It is also possible to have *too much* self-confidence. When someone's self-image gets inflated, it can negatively affect the way they act around others and may even lead to their downfall. A gorilla might huff and puff its chest all it wants, but without real strength, it is sure to lose a battle. This is the same for human's sense of self-confidence. If we let compliments get to our heads, we may start acting overly snobbish and over-estimate our abilities. How prone are you to this? Describe a recent compliment you received that boosted your self-confidence.

For You:

Don't be shy with this question. You might have a timid view of yourself or don't like tooting your own horn, but let it out. How do other people perceive you? What compliments stand out to you? It could be a simple compliment about your outfit.

How did you feel when you heard the compliment? If your love language relies on words of affirmation, then compliments are known to be your highest form of love that you receive from others.[8.3] Explain to your partner how this compliment made you feel and how it altered your sense of self.

Describe a recent compliment you received that boosted your self-confidence.

Did it make you feel like you could do anything? Did it make you feel accepted? Did it make you feel like a different person?

For Your Partner:

This is your time to probe! For most of your day, you might be naïve to the way others see your partner. You see them through your perspective alone. With this question, however, you get to see your partner how others see them. How much do others appreciate your partner?

Granted, their answer to this question is still filtered through your partner's interpretation of the compliment, but this gives at least a little bit more outside perspective. And the more you can see about your partner, remember, the easier it is to understand what makes them happy.

On a deeper level, this question helps you determine how influential compliments might be and how much it defines your partner's self-confidence. For example, if your partner sounds appreciative and humble about this compliment, it's safe to assume they are level-headed in their self-image. However, if they start to explain just how life-changing and eye-opening a particular compliment was (verging on that "too-much" side of the self-confidence spectrum), you might begin to notice just how reliant they are on compliments. It's here that you need to be wary and cautious and is the heart of this question.

For You Both:

Compliments are the easiest way to determine just how reliant you are on others' opinions. As a couple, you must remind each other how much you are worth without bending over backwards for praise. Let go of this need for external validation.

This is especially true during your wedding. There's a certain sense of over-bearing confidence that I see some grooms have in their ability to stay emotionless around their groomsmen. It's almost like there's some sort of unwritten code saying you must show overt confidence in your ability to not cry in front of people. But when it's just the groom and partner alone, they let their full emotions show and tears start running. That's what you need. The excessive acting around your friends is just the need for external validation and hurts the sincerity of your films and photographs. Let your true self come out.

Instead of building yourselves based on others' opinions, focus on building your self-confidence on the foundation of the love you have for one another.

Follow-up Questions:

Q140. On a scale of 1 to 10, how much do you let compliments inflate your ego?

Q141. Describe how a recent compliment changed your thoughts about yourself?

Q142. On a scale of 1 to 10, how much appreciated do you feel by others?

Q143. What compliments make you the happiest?

Q144. True or false: your mood is heavily reliant on others' praise.

Describe a recent compliment you received that boosted your self-confidence.

Q145. When are you most at peace?

The wedding day flew by. The groom and bride had a stunning ceremony and were now happily eating through their reception meals. We were all in a beautiful Italian-style banquet hall, surrounded by the newlywed's closest family and friends.

I started to prepare for the wedding speeches when I realized the groom's mother wasn't in attendance. The couple explained that she wasn't the most supportive of her son's relationship and new wife. Drama among family members is not uncommon, and I've seen a couple of soap opera plotlines play out behind the scenes of weddings.

In the middle of the speeches, the groom's aunt made her way to the podium and announced she had a letter to read. It was from the groom's mother.

"I promise to love you because you understand what's behind those sparkling eyes of his like I do. You understand what he means when he talks from his heart but gets all messed up. And you laugh at his jokes the way I do. And how could I not love the person that loves all that about my son?

On this day I'm so very proud. I'm proud of the person my little boy turned into. I'm proud of the person he has chosen to spend his days with. And I'm proud to be his mom."

This letter struck me as a perfect example of what acceptance and coming to peace can look like. In the letter, the groom's mother had finally accepted the bride and her son's choice. She came to terms with the present moment and allowing it to be.

You can hold opinions and judgements about things that you don't like, but it isn't until you accept these realities that you can begin to feel at peace. When are you most at peace?

For You:

The purpose of this question is to help you understand what brings you peace and how to find peace to overcome hostile moments. Describe three different moments that have brought you into a sense of ease and explain why.

"I felt most at peace laying by the water because..."

"I felt most at peace curled up with a book because..."

"I felt most at peace eating with my grandparents because..."

Then, describe a moment of peace you would like to happen in the future. It could be a trip to Fiji, a picnic in the park, cuddling on the couch with a book. Name and explain three different scenarios you believe will bring you a sense of peace.

For Your Partner:

Remember these six moments about your partner, and it will be easy to promote these same feelings of peace in the future. You'll notice a pattern in settings, people, and actions during the moments they describe. Keep track of what your partner is doing in all these moments. There may be a pattern in the setting (e.g. a relaxing breeze) or the company (e.g. their elementary school friends), but it is their actions that lead to peace.

It is only in themselves, without a reliance on the people or places around them, that true peace can be felt. So, what are they doing when they let this peace overtake them? Remember their answer, and help them get into a similar activity when negativity starts to creep in.

For You Both:

Peace can be synonymous with acceptance. The acceptance of a situation promotes inner peace, and inner peace allows for an acceptance of a situation. Again, I know it can sound a little woo-woo but let me explain this while summing up all The Five A's.

When you start to feel anxious, or avoidant, or disorganized around your partner, the only way back to secure attachment is accepting reality for what it is. And that reality is a shared love. Trust each other's attachment to each other. Accept your affection.

When you start to feel obstacles holding you back from your goals around your partner, the only way to your achievement is accepting reality for what it is. And that reality is a shared love. Trust each other's drive and motivation to grow together. Accept your ambition.

When you start to feel criticized for your ideas around your partner, the only way to mutually appreciate each other is accepting reality for what it is. And that reality is a shared love. Trust that you have each other's best interests at heart, even in conflict. Accept your artistry.

When you start to feel out of place or too unfamiliar around your partner, the only way to feel a shared experience is accepting reality for what it is. And that reality is a shared love. Trust that you both want to understand each other's beliefs and take the time to learn from and with each other. Accept your awareness.

And when you start to feel downgraded or understated as a human being around your partner, the only way back to a healthy self-confidence is accepting reality for what it is. And that reality is a shared love. Trust that you are enough and that you don't need excessive external validation to deserve love. You are complete as a couple, but also complete as an individual. Accept your awakening.

Follow-up Questions:

Q146. What do you think about when you want to relax?

Q147. Describe three past events when you felt the most at peace.

Q148. Describe three scenarios that would bring you into peace.

Q149. If money wasn't a question, what would you do every day?

Q150. Why do you love your partner?

"On the surface, acceptance looks like a passive state, but in reality it is active and creative because it brings something entirely new into this world. That peace, that subtle energy vibration, is consciousness, and one of the ways in which it enters this world is through surrendered action, one aspect of which is acceptance.

If you can neither enjoy or bring acceptance to what you do– stop. Otherwise, you are not taking responsibility for the only thing you can really take responsibility for, which also happens to be one thing that really matters: your state of consciousness. And if you are not taking responsibility for your state of consciousness, you are not taking responsibility for life."

– Eckhart Tolle.

And now, you have a responsibility for your life and your partner's. Protect it.

STOP – Before moving forward:

How would you rate your element of awakening?

☐ ☐ ☐ ☐ ☐ ☐ ☐ ☐ ☐ ☐
1 2 3 4 5 6 7 8 9 10

How would you rate your partner's element of awakening?

☐ ☐ ☐ ☐ ☐ ☐ ☐ ☐ ☐ ☐
1 2 3 4 5 6 7 8 9 10

Rapid Action Steps:

1. Write down the number one area in your life that needs the most improvement with your element of awakening (e.g. - forgiving, letting go, accepting).

2. Every morning for the next week, wake up and tell yourself that you are going to act with a better awakening.

3. Love relentlessly.

SECTION III
CONCLUSION

9. CONCLUSION

Congratulations on making it to the end of this book. If you went through the questions with your partner, I truly hope the journey of discussions has helped shed light on your unique personality. If you went through this book alone, I hope you've witnessed just how extraordinary you are on every level. The Five A's are in all of us, but they have a special structure inside of you. It is this unique mixture of elements that make you and your partner, quite literally, fit perfectly together.

You can think of The Five A's as different sides to a five-sided puzzle piece. Each side is characterized and shaped very distinctly, depending on how you were raised and how you think today. You have unique shapes to your cog-like puzzle, and with the right person, the sides of your personality fit perfectly together as they rotate together in sync. When you master each of The Five A's, it becomes increasingly easier to strengthen your attachment to your partner.

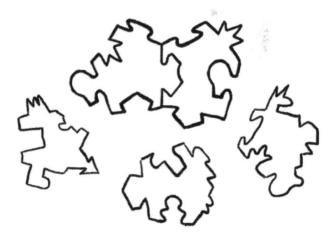

You are now equipped to master each element every day in your relationship, preparing for your wedding and beyond. There is nothing more fulfilling than a relationship that cultivates growth in all five elements.

Affection: This element explores your early childhood. Throughout the chapter, you learned how your past relationships affect your attachment styles to others in the present.

Ambition: This element guides you towards achieving your goals. You now understand what drives and motivates you toward success in your personal life and relationship.

Artistry: This element defines your work ethic and creativity in your careers. You now know how your professional life translates to your relationship, and how you create value, handle criticism, and engage in conflict resolution.

Awareness: This element is your affinity to connect. Throughout the chapter, you learned to appreciate other people and how metaprograms can influence behaviours and create biases.

Awakening: This element is the through-line between all of the elements and stages in your life. You now know that positivity starts within you, and acceptance of the present moment is the very first step to positivity.

Conclusion

All of The Five A's are imperative to your whole being. These elements make up who you are, and they define how you behave with your partner in the world. But did you notice a hidden theme? A deeper meaning?

I wrote this book to help you and your partner prepare for your wedding smiles and a lifetime of marriage, but I hope you caught onto the deeper meaning behind these learning moments and conversations as well.

When you spot this hidden lesson, and if you let it manifest into your five elements, your entire being will be at peace. You will find that your mood is calmer, your days are lighter, and your interactions are all magical.

This will happen because it is meant to happen.

People often say everything happens for a reason, but I like to say everything happens for a cause. You didn't come across this book without reason. You read it because you were meant to read it.

The Five A's are not a new concept, they are subconsciously inside each of us, and this book has merely articulated them into words and connected them to existing theories and observations about the human psyche. The Five A's are in your spirit, they will guide you as an individual, a loving couple, and a compassionate member of society.

The pages in this book are meant for you to reference again and again. As you continue to revisit the discussions inspired by this book, the hidden meaning will find its way to you and your partner.

But when you finish reading this page, it is the next chapters that matter most. What you make of this book will be found in the next questions you ask, the next discussions you have, and the next experiences you create. Above anything else, remember that your smile has a bigger impact than you think, and your internal theatre is meant to be a place of positivity.

For the future, I wish you nothing but endless love.

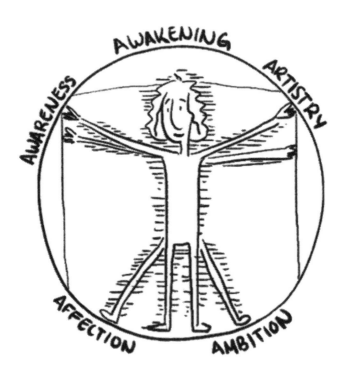

10. ALL QUESTIONS

AFFECTION:

Q1. Who made you feel the safest while growing up?

Q2. What was it about this person or these people that made you feel safe?

Q3. What are the top three characteristics of this person that you want in your partner?

Q4. How would you describe this person's approach to cultivating your sense of safety?

Q5. What action made you feel safe?

Q6. Describe a specific memory of how this person made you feel safe.

Q7. When you needed help, how often did you ask for help?

Q8. Describe an early memory where you under stress and had to solve a problem on your own.

Q9. If possible, describe something you were taught as a child that you felt had unsatisfactory guidance.

Q10. Share a specific memory of when you needed the most help from someone else.

Q11. Practice the Corrective Experience exercise.

Q12. Clearly invite your partner to feel an empathic pain or stress you currently have and accept that they are there to help.

Q13. When did you feel anxious in your relationships?

Q14. Would you describe yourself as overly frightened when your caregivers were unavailable?

Q15. Was there a lot of unpredictability during your childhood?

Q16. Thinking back, do you remember being overly obsessive about certain things as a child? Explain.

Q17. If applicable, describe a childhood memory that still makes you angry today.

Q18. What reoccurring events happen when you feel anxious today? Describe these patterns to your partner, as well as how you can implement an abundance mindset to mitigate this feeling.

Q19. Is there anyone you were really close with, but now feel confused about how they treated you?

Q20. Are you still holding on to these confusing childhood relationships?

Q21. Describe a childhood memory of yourself actively going into a dangerous situation.

Q22. What one situation, in your early childhood, caused you to feel the most loved one second, followed by the most hurt the next second?

Q23. When do you feel the most frozen to act on stressful situations?

Q24. Come up with a secret code that you and your partner can use to indicate the other is slipping into a behaviour of insecurity.

Q25. Where in the world would you like to live?

Q26. On a scale of 1 to 10, how happy are you with the attachment style you believe to have?

Q27. On a scale of 1 to 10, how much do you think you need to work on your attachment with your partner?

Q28. Describe a pleasant environment you frequently visited as a child.

Q29. How clearly can you see your partner in your dream home?

Q30. On a scale of 1 to 10, how flexible do you believe yourself to be when it comes to meeting your partner's needs in a future home?

AMBITION:

Q31. Who was living the life you wanted to live?

Q32. Do you believe you set goals too much for the short-term or for the long-term?

Q33. Were you trying to be like too many people?

Q34. Thinking back, do you think you were confused about the look of success and what you believe to be success today?

Q35. How easy was it to achieve the goals you wanted?

Q36. In what grade school situations would you have liked your idol to take over for you?

Q37. What aspects of yourself do you wish you worked on more?

Q38. Do you believe it was hard for you to determine what stopped you from achieving your goals?

Q39. Do you think you handled your problems well?

Q40. What stopped you from achieving your goals as a young adult?

Q41. When you are stuck on a problem, do you often to think about it first, or act right away?

Q42. How easy is it for you to share your problems with your partner?

Q43. How would you have utilized a Think Week as a grade school student?

Q44. How much do you think you've grown at identifying the true causes of your problems?

Q45. Do you believe you would use a Think Week effectively today?

Q46. How often did you confuse surface-level barriers with deep-rooted barriers as grade-schooler? Do you think you are better at it today?

Q47. Use the Socratic method to determine a deep-rooted problem that you have about your wedding.

Q48. Design a 7-day schedule for a hypothetical Think Week to design your perfect wedding celebration.

Q49. Which of these methods of thinking were you most familiar with: divergent thinking or convergent thinking?

Q50. Which form of thinking do you tend towards while working on group projects?

Q51. In your relationship, do you believe you take on the same or different methods of thinking?

Q52. Does traditional education keep you from solving problems by divergently thinking? Would you say you can think creatively?

Q53. Would you say you can smoothly transition into divergent thinking?

Q54. Go through your wedding day schedule (or a hypothetical wedding day schedule) and come up with a creative way to get in all the important events you want with at least 15 minutes of leeway time between them. Pro tip—treat driving to locations as an event.

Q55. When are you in flow state?

Q56. Do you still experience the same flow-state you did as a child? Is it better today?

Q57. What are you doing when you lose track of time?

Q58. Do you lose track of time doing similar things? Totally different things?

Q59. What tasks do you need to do, but also know that your partner would do them better?

Q60. If you had to do one job for the rest of your life, what would it be?

ARTISTRY:

Q61. How do you bring value in your profession?

Q62. On a scale of 1 to 10, how much do you believe your professional colleagues understand your worth?

Q63. What topics tend to make you the most argumentative in your relationship?

Q64. Why is your job special to you?

Q65. What do you appreciate the most about your profession?

Q66. Which values around work do you and your partner share the most?

Q67. Why do you think your coworkers like talking to you?

Q68. Who are the work friends you enjoy being around? Why?

Q69. On a scale of 1 to 10, how open are you to listening to their ideas?

Q70. When do you most validate your coworkers' ideas? When are you least validating?

Q71. How intimidating do you think you are around your colleagues?

Q72. Who are three people you speak differently to? Explain why.

Q73. Describe who you look up to in your industry.

Q74. On a scale of 1 to 10, how engaged are you at trying to persuade your coworkers?

Q75. Do you believe you persuade your significant other drastically different than your coworkers?

Q76. What do you think your partner will appreciate most about your role model? Least?

Q77. How defensive would you get if your partner disagreed with your role-model?

Q78. Who is someone you dislike in your industry? Explain why.

Q79. On a scale of 1 to 10, how assertive do you think you are?

Q80. How often do you fight for your ideas in the workplace?

Q81. Would your colleagues describe you more of going over-the-top in proposing new projects, or someone who retracts at the first word of disagreement?

Q82. When do you tend to sacrifice your initial ideas?

Q83. Describe a recent argument that caused you to compromise a lot.

Q84. True or false: you tend to fight to be right before mutual agreement.

Q85. When do you feel the most accomplished and fulfilled?

Q86. Do you believe you have a validating, volatile, or avoidant conflict resolution style with your partner?

Q87. How often do you dwell on arguments you've had to compromise on?

Q88. What ethics are you absolutely not willing to compromise on in your work life?

Q89. When do you feel the most passion for your line of work?

Q90. Which highly-rewarding tasks at work do you believe you can do for your relationship as well (e.g. organizing schedules, reading finances, décor choice)?

AWARENESS:

Q91. If you could reimagine your birth, what would it look like?

Q92. Who do you think has the most influence in the world today?

Q93. On a scale of 1 to 10, how strongly would you have wished to be raised differently?

Q94. Why do you think your birth into the world was perfect for you?

Q95. Why do you think your birth into the world was completely wrong for you?

Q96. Do you actively stay up to date with general world knowledge?

Q97. Where in the world do you think you best fit in?

Q98. How do you typically lose track of time while surfing the internet?

Q99. What cultural phenomenon are you currently interested in?

Q100. List your top three dream places to live in

Q101. Which of your travels sparked the most engagement in you and your partner?

Q102. Complete this sentence: "I feel accepted where I am now because…"

Q103. When planning a trip, do you fill your schedule or do you leave it open?

Q104. Do you act based on external proof or your own intuition?

Q105. What motivates you to buy certain foods?

Q106. Describe a recent moment you let this meta-program influence you into making a regrettable decision.

Q107. Do you think you are easily influenced?

Q108. When was the last time you completely disagreed with your partner? Was this due to one of you having an external proof meta-program while the other used their own intuition?

Q109. When in all of history, other than right now, would you have liked to live?

Q110. Was your last big purchase made out of fear or out of pleasure?

Q111. Do you believe you make more decisions to relieve pain or to gain pleasure?

Q112. List your top five reasons for wanting a one-way time travel ticket.

Q113. Complete this sentence: "I want to live during a time where I can…"

Q114. When thinking of your wedding schedule, what times do you believe will cause the most pain? What will cause the most pleasure?

Q115. Why do you, or why don't you, feel connected enough in the world?

Q116. Do you notice how similar you are, or do you notice how dissimilar you are around others?

Q117. On a scale of 1 to 10, how comfortable do you feel around the people you spend the most time with as a couple?

Q118. What groups of people do you feel the most connected with?

Q119. How often do you make decisions based on how different they are?

Q120. In what situations do you like seeing similarities, and what situations do you like seeing differences?

AWAKENING:

Q121. Describe an embarrassing moment that still makes you shiver.

Q122. What types of memories embarrass you the most?

Q123. How often do you believe to be in a depressive state?

Q124. Describe an embarrassing moment that makes you laugh.

Q125. Predict and describe a future embarrassing moment that includes your partner.

Q126. What do you tend to think to yourself when you feel embarrassed?

Q127. What upcoming event are you most frightened of?

Q128. Describe doing something you know would be difficult for you to do.

Q129. What are the worst (realistic) consequences that could happen?

Q130. Remind yourself and your partner why you are going through this in the first place?

Q131. What are the best-case scenarios that could happen because of this happening?

Q132. What makes you excited for your future with your partner?

Q133. What upcoming event are you most excited for?

Q134. What do you feel like you lack the most in your life?

Q135. What excites you the most for your upcoming wedding?

Q136. Describe a past excitement that caused you to only think about that event all the time.

Q137. Do you believe you are too distracted when you think of upcoming exciting events?

Q138. What are you most thankful for right now?

Q139. Describe a recent compliment you received that boosted your self-confidence.

Q140. On a scale of 1 to 10, how much do you let compliments inflate your ego?

Q141. Describe how a recent compliment changed your thoughts about yourself?

Q142. On a scale of 1 to 10, how appreciated do you feel by others?

Q143. What compliments make you the happiest?

Q144. True or false: your mood is heavily reliant on others' praise.

Q145. When are you most at peace?

Q146. What do you think about when you want to relax?

Q147. Describe three past events when you felt the most at peace.

Q148. Describe three scenarios that would bring you into peace.

Q149. If money wasn't a question, what would you do every day?

Q150. Why do you love your partner?

Wedding Day Confidence

ACKNOWLEDGEMENTS

To The Editor:

Dear Razan,

I cannot thank you enough for bringing wisdom to these pages. Your feedback on my original book plan has helped me more than you know. From a skeleton to more concrete thoughts and a solid plan of action, you have been the guide any author would aspire to have at their side. Your expertise with the word and your endless insight has ornamented these pages with charming vigour. Not to mention your candour and sincerity, traits that I'm appreciative you brought to this project and to the ultimate benefit of readers .

Out of everything, though, I truly believe it is your growing curiosity that deserves the highest recognition. On my first approach, you welcomed my thoughts with open arms and an open mind to match. Unpacking my ideas, diving into your research, and bringing your own experiences to the mix; these pages are only as valuable as they are because of your essential creativity and curiosity. Not only is this a sign of a beautiful mind, but an invaluable friend. Taking on this book in the middle of 2020 could not have been easy, and I owe its strength to you.

To The Illustrator:

Dear Sam,

We have been through thick and thin in our creative endeavours, and I could not have anyone else paint these pages. Your artistry amazes me every day, and your character is one of magnificence. Everything you touch becomes magical, and every conversation becomes impassioned. Not only do your illustrative pieces touch lives, but the loving message you constantly spread is unmatched. I am proud to call you family.

To The Friends and Family:

Dear Friends and Family,

I come to tears of joy when I reread these pages. When I envision the healthy relationships that this book aims to cultivate, your loving eyes and your loving words are omnipresent. Every chapter and every question were built upon my experiences with you, and it is your matched affection that becomes the goal I wish for every reader.

Mom and dad, you set the bar for the kindness and love I believe the world should strive for. Amanda and Adrian are the wonderful outcomes of this bar. We owe everything to you.

Lola and Lolo, you raised me with an unrelenting love I never quite understood as a child. I'm unsure I'll ever understand how strong this love is for all your grandchildren. All I know is that I am proud to know you will always be at my side. You are part of me; I take on the world through your hardworking hands, and I see it all with your analytical eyes. But most of all, it is your idea of treating everyone like family that I will embrace with dignity.

Highway 8 to Main. There are too many of us and too many we've welcomed into our arms to mention, but you know who you are. From Mountain View to Orchard Park and beyond McMaster University, you've touched my heart in more ways than I can ever say. Although each of us has grown exceptionally on different paths, our memories together are forever within reach. You all are the epitome of secure kinship, and I know for a fact that nothing in my life would be as wonderful as it is without you all. We may not be as free for a summer joyride as we used to be, but I cherish knowing that we are just one phone call or text away when needed. You will always have my back and heart.

To The Team:

Dear Brian,

I'm not sure I say this enough, or at all, but you are a pivotal part of everything that is, was, and can be. Not just in relation to the artwork we create at every wedding, but in all aspects of creative business and the pursuit of art on a global scale. You are destined for more than you think, whatever that may be. On every path you find yourself on, know that your back is covered.

Dear Vincent,

Fortunately, we were friends before we got into this camera business thing. This can also be a downside. As much as I believe that people who work together should be good friends, I also believe we let it get to us sometimes. At least I do. The biggest regret I have in anything is critiquing your work on impulse. I know we say things jokingly and on friendly terms, thus the downfall of being such close friends, but I do wish I could take it back. You are creative in so many ways, and you have been the foundation to anything I've had the privilege of being part of. I owe a lot to you, both professionally and personally. Remember that on every path you find yourself on, your back is covered.

Dear Prince,

In the amount of time we've known each other, I've seen you conquer the lows and lift up others at the highs. Your true smile is worth looking up to, and you are a real one to fall back on in times of need. I don't know how you manage to handle all the challenges and all the hurdles, but what I do know is that I am so proud to call you a brother. We both know there are higher powers elevating everything we do, and I feel it most when we team-up. I'm unsure of the exact vision, but you are destined to keep following this path. If ever you need, know that your back is covered.

Dear Francis,

You are the ace up anyone's sleeve. You teach me things I never thought I'd need to know, and you shine light where I never thought was dark. In everything you do, you bring a positive spark and it shows in all the magic you share. Not just with the camera, but with your kind touch and warm words. I know you are on the precipice of something big, and I know you feel that too. Thank you for always being there. Don't let go of your visions, because whatever path you find yourself on, your back is covered.

To My Mentors:

Dear Riccardo,

One day, I was walking along the sandy ocean shore alone. I was in the middle of a video-related problem, and I knew no one could really understand and recognize the help I needed. Then I thought of you and your cheerful voice of encouragement.

In my head, I thought of the advice you might give me. With my feet buried in the sand, I imagined your friendly voice telling me what to do. Telling me the questions I should be asking myself and guiding me to what you believe would be the best solution for me. I know it was just my imagination, but it was clear as day. Just like the memories of our unforgettable Osmosis Workshop days.

In all your efforts to bring up the wedding filmmaking community, I really believe the most important part is in your warmth. You approach everyone and everything with undeniable love, and it shows in the magic you produce. Your authenticity is something anyone should strive for, and it is something I think about every time I press record. I am still star-struck to know that we are friends. Thank you for your constant support and guidance.

Dear Remi,

In many ways, you embody the ultimate goal of any professional artist, me included. I'm privileged enough to say that I found your social media page quite a few years ago, and I've witnessed your growth as both an artistic and business mind. And on top of this professional growth, your family has grown in the midst of it all. I'm sure I can say this on behalf of any family man that you are a figure to look up to.

Balancing home, creative, and business life is a challenge that does not go unseen, and your execution with Octoa is something I'm proud to immerse myself in. For any creativepreneur who spends the time reading these acknowledgements, I hope you can come across Remi's path as I did.

Remi, your kind and professional (but also humorous and welcoming) attitude is one I will always be happy to think back to. Thank you for your constant support and guidance.

Dear Richard,

I don't believe anyone from Canada visits the UK and thinks about surfing. But now I do. Your personal stories of growth and empowerment are an inspiration to many and are my constant reminders to keep striving for more and to always aim for better.

If there's one thing I think back to about your outstanding Clarity Workshop, it is your stance on security. In many ways, your principles around feeling safe and confident are riddled through this book. Feeling secure enough to have choices and to stick up for yourself is such a universal idea. I would not have made that connection between business and meaningful relationships had it not been for your lessons.

Thank you for welcoming me into your community of like-minded creatives and thank you for your constant support and guidance.

To My Couples:

This project would not be what it is without the couples who helped shape the ideas and experiences mentioned. The gossip, the tears, and the moments of undeniable love will forever be ingrained in me, and that is truly an honour for anyone to have. I don't have enough thank-you's to give to all the couples I've had the pleasure to work with, so please take these pages as my form of respects to you all. You also have my contact if you ever need anything.

To The Girl Who Replied To My Instagram Story:

Dear Bebe,

I'm writing this in the final hours before launching this book. Last minute, very wedding-speech of me. And as every best man or maid of honour says, get ready for the gushy part:

I can't begin to verbalize the feelings you give me.

From a fluttering heart during our first text conversations, and now an even deeper warmth every time I see your smile. Out of every book I've read, every wedding witnessed and every written word I can fathom, nothing defines love the way you do.

A calming touch. A trusting hug. A twinkling smile. And peaceful words of devotion.

Thank you for always being the guiding light on this road we're on, and thank you for continuing to bring out the five a's in me and everything we do.

ACKNOWLEDGEMENTS

Thinking back, it was our very first conversation that sparked the beginnings of this book, playing truth or truth. Between your classes, our work shifts, and my video editing routines, some of our deepest questions and aspirations came out of us. If I could add a 151st question in this book, it would be one of the first questions we asked each other:

Q151. What is your perfect day?

Back then, I said my perfect day required you. Now, I can say every day is my perfect day with you.

About The Author

My name is Aaron, and I created Aaron Daniel Films to empower those in love. I'm a wedding filmmaker sharing what love looks like in the modern world, and the magic it creates. For the couple and individual, and for the artistic minds who understand that the greatest masterpieces in life grow from an understanding of love.

AaronDanielFilms.com shares your real wedding stories on film, and explains how this love came to be through the blog.

I'm an Ontario-based wedding videographer and blogger specializing in helping couples create their best, candid and natural moments on camera.

After personally learning from the world's top wedding filmmakers – from Italy, to the United Kingdom, Poland, the Netherlands and the United States – it gives me great joy to provide my artistic expertise to Ontario, Canada and beyond. These experiences have undoubtedly led me to the privileged recognition by wedding leaders like Junebug Weddings, Worldwide Event Videographers Association, and Looks Like Film to name a few.

The reason I continue to write and publish about human relationship is because it is my go-to method of directing. When a couple is directed based on their emotional connection, the more true and raw the film becomes. They emit a genuine smile to all things around them, act with noticeable kindness, and are reminiscent of what only top Hollywood actors can embody.

Art and love are one and the same. If you know one, you know the other. That is the fuel that drives Aaron Daniel Films.

It is my job as your wedding filmmaker to make this come true.

If you are planning to get married soon, it would be a pleasure to help create your wedding film heirloom for generations to enjoy. You can get in contact and follow along using the links below.

I can't wait to hear from you!

Until next time,

- A

AaronDanielFilms.com

Instagram.com/AaronDanielFilms

Facebook.com/AaronDanielFilms

Youtube.com/c/AaronDanielFilms

Notes and References

2.1 - Navarro, Joe, and Marvin Karlins. *What Every Body Is Saying: An Ex-Fbi Agent's Guide to Speed Reading People.* New York, NY: HarperCollins, 2008. Print. This was a phenomenal book to give a foundational understanding about reading people's verbal communication. Navarro's teachings has greatly helped read the rooms of many wedding waiting rooms and reception halls.

2.2 – Navarro, Joe. *Dating: Body Language Basics.* 2011. Much like his other works, I found this very intriguing and a wonderful quick reference book for anyone to pick up and understand. I use his work in a lot of my directing, mainly while observing and determining how to best direct people in front of the camera.

2.3 – Zola. https://www.zola.com/expert-advice/5-effective-ways-to-fight-wedding-planning-stress

2.4 – Gottman, John, and Nan Silver. *Why Marriages Succeed or Fail: And How to Make Yours Last.* 2014. Print. Gottman's work has always been intriguing to me. I see his work being cited throughout many wedding and relationship blogs, and for good reason. I believe it is the old science student in me who longs for longitudinal studies across the wedding industry and marriage culture.

2.5 – Tyng, Chai M et al. "The Influences of Emotion on Learning and Memory." *Frontiers in psychology* vol. 8 1454. 24 Aug. 2017, doi:10.3389/fpsyg.2017.01454

2.6 - Tomkins, S., & Smith, B. (1995). Script theory. In E. Demos (Ed.), *Exploring Affect: The Selected Writings of Silvan S Tomkins* (Studies in Emotion and Social Interaction, pp. 312-388). Cambridge: Cambridge University Press. doi:10.1017/CBO9780511663994.021

4.1 – Ainsworth, M. D., & Bell, S. M. (1970). Attachment, exploration, and separation: Illustrated by the behavior of one-year-olds in a strange situation. *Child Development, 41*(1), 49–67. https://doi.org/10.2307/1127388

4.2 - Main, M., & Solomon, J. (1990). Procedures for identifying infants as disorganized/disoriented during the Ainsworth Strange Situation. In M.T. Greenberg, D. Cicchetti & E.M. Cummings (Eds.), *Attachment in the Preschool Years* (pp. 121–160). Chicago, University of Chicago Press.

4.3 - Levine, Amir, and Rachel Heller. *Attached: The New Science of Adult Attachment and How It Can Help You Find and Keep-Love.* 2011. Print.

4.4 - Heller, Diane P. *The Power of Attachment: How to Create Deep and Lasting Intimate Relationships.* 2019. Print.

4.5 - Johnson, Sue. *Love Sense: The Revolutionary New Science of Romantic Relationships.* London: Piatkus, 2014. Print. This was actually my first book that I delved into about the science of love. In 2018, I tried my hand at doing a vlog series talking about her work. It didn't catch, so I started writing about it instead.

5.1 - Dalio, Ray. *Principles.* New York, NY: Simon and Schuster, 2017. Print. I absolutely love this book. It is both a phenomenal reference book to come back to (much like a manual for running an organization) as well as a personal story of Dalio's life. I think back to this book quite often and recommend it to almost any entrepreneur.

5.2 – De Jesus, Marino. *Living Within My Life Frame: My Destiny To Be What I Am.* Hamilton, ON: Xlibris Corp, 2013. Print. It's a little funny referencing my own name. My last name to be exact. My grandfather has, and will remain, a true inspiration to my family and I. I retell his story through both his published book's words as well as his personal stories to his grandchildren. He was also a frequent writer for the Hamilton Spectator (newspaper), so if you are interested in more of his writing, his book is sure to delight.

5.3 – Think Week: https://www.wsj.com/articles/SB1111966625830690477

5.4 - Gottman, John M, and Nan Silver. *The Seven Principles for Making Marriage Work.* London: Cassell Illustrated, 2018. Print.

5.5 - Csikszentmihalyi, Mihaly. (1990). Flow: The Psychology of Optimal Experience. You can also find a modern and summarized understanding here, https://positivepsychology.com/mihaly-csikszentmihalyi-father-of-flow/, written by Mike Oppland, BA, MBA

5.6 - Guilford, J.P. *The Nature of Human Intelligence.* New York: McGraw-Hill, 1967.

6.1 – Fasoli, Riccardo. *Osmosis Workshop.* Kreativ Wedding: Germany, 2019. Both Riccardo and Remi (mentioned next), are the two individuals I look to most when it comes to wedding filmmaking. Riccardo has such a fantastic way of positioning his personality into his work, and is well-deserving of the praise he gets in the international wedding filmmaking community.

6.2 – Schouten, Remi. *Osmosis Workshop.* Maru Films: Amsterdam, The Netherlands, 2019. Remi is an extraordinary wedding filmmaker, and deserves just as much respect as Riccardo. At the time of writing, he has also just launched his international CRM system, Octoa. I am a user and absolutely love the work him and his team does to help the wedding filmmaking community. I would be hard pressed to invest in a company that doesn't fully understand my industry's needs like Remi does.

6.3 - Gottman, John, and Nan Silver. *Why Marriages Succeed or Fail: And How to Make Yours Last.* 2014. Print. I just reused this reference, but gave it a new listing for this new chapter. Easier organization and reference.

7.1 – Metaprograms: https://blog.iqmatrix.com/meta-programs. There are mainstream web pages that explain what meta-programs are. This is just one of many.

7.2 – Pignataro, Carlo. *Sell With Style: The ultimate guide to luxury selling.* 2018. Carlo is such a wonderful person to hear from. I am a huge fan of his podcast, Lux and Tech, and can listen to his insights and questions all day. This book, as well as his second book, Serve With Style, should be a staple in sales associate's arsenal. He really helped me understand what it takes to bring your delicate and valuable relationships to the next level.

8.1 - Tolle, Eckhart. *A New Earth: Awakening to Your Life's Purpose.* London: Penguin Book, 2018. Print.

8.2 – Tolle, Eckhart. *The Power Of Now: A Guide To Spiritual Enlightenment.* Vancouver, Canada: Namaste Publishing Inc., 1997. Print. Tolle's books are those you must read over and over, at varying times of your life. In every hurdle you encounter, this book will teach you something new, and show you a better perspective on whatever it is you are struggling with. Tolle is a spiritual guide I hope to come across one day, solely to give thanks.

8.3 - Chapman, Gary D. *The 5 Love Languages.* Chicago: Northfield Pub, 2015. Print. The five love languages are a staple in every wedding vendors communication process. I really believe everyone should fall back to Chapman's ideas and implement them into both personal and professional relationships.

A

Manufactured by Amazon.ca
Bolton, ON